THE TAMILIAN ANTIQUARY

THE
TAMILIAN ANTIQUARY

Editor

PANDIT D. SAVARIROYAN

VOL – I

NO – VI

GYAN

Published by

GYAN

Gyan Publishing House
5, Ansari Road
Daryaganj, New Delhi-110002
Phone: 011-47034999, 9811692060
E-mail: books@gyanbooks.com

Distribution Network
gyanbooks.com
India, USA, Canada, UK, Australia, France

ISBN : 978-81-212-3061-2 (PB)
First Published, 1910

2nd Impression 2020

Printed at: Gyan Press, Delhi.

The book at your disposal is the edition of an old book originally published long back. The Text quality of this book may not be at par as compared to our other books but many readers approached us to reprint this important book so that it could satiate their hunger. We request all the readers of this book to help us to improve its quality by providing the necessary text of those pages which are not properly visible. Your valuable support in this case will be highly appreciated and acknowledged and our future readers will be benefitted immensely.

THE
TAMILIAN ANTIQUARY.

PURA-PORUL, "THE OBJECTIVE".

A SUMMARISED ACCOUNT OF

BY

The late Rev. Dr. G. U. POPE, M A., D.D.

WITH AN INTRODUCTION BY

J. M. NALLASVĀMI PILLAI, B.A., B.L.,

District Munsiff, Rajahmundry, (Godavari Dt.)

PUBLISHED BY

THE HONORARY SECRETARY, T. A. SOCIETY,

TRICHINOPOLY.

MADRAS:

PRINTED AT THE MEYKANDAN PRESS,

1910.

INTRODUCTION.

THE extracts from Pura-porul Venbā-Mālai and Puranānūru was originally published in the 'Asiatic Quarterly Review' and the 'Indian Antiquary' respectively and were sent to me by the late Rev. Dr. G. U. Pope, for publication in the 'Light of Truth or the Siddhānta Dīpikā,' and most of them were accordingly printed in the earlier volumes of this Magazine. They are now reprinted in book-form so as to be available to all students of Tamil. Dr. Pope's contributions to Tamil literature have been various and immense, and published in a number of Magazines, besides his large editions of 'Kural' and 'Nāladiyār', 'Tiruvāçakam' and Tamil Text-books and Tamil Grammar, and in his last days he had prepared a translation of Palamoli about which he wrote to me and which he valued highly. He had revised his Kural and Nāladiyār also. Dr. Pope's son Mr. John V. Pope, who is now in India, has kindly promised to send me all the collected papers and it is my intention to publish them from time to time; and it is hoped that this present *brochure* will serve to whet the appetite of the Tamil public for the more that is to come.

I was in correspondence with the late Dr. Pope about bringing out an adequate account of his life and works and he wrote to me to say that he left this duty to be performed by his sons, and Mr. J. V. Pope has kindly undertaken this pious duty and has promised to send me instalments of the 'life' from June next and this I hope to publish in the Siddhānta Dīpikā.

Dr. Pope was a genuine scholar and worked hard till the last days of his long life. Being possessed of a generous heart he helped every one who came to him for help. The consequence was, he lived poor and died poor.

He fulfilled the ideal of the ancient Tamiḻ poets who would rather starve than beg, and who lived for fame alone. He loved Tamiḻ literature with all his heart and he rated it very highly and wanted to be inscribed in his tombstone as a student of Tamiḻ. He spoke of the 'Kuṟaḷ' as a book unparallelled in the literature of any country or nation. He wrote to me to say, "Professor Max Müller has contrived to get a great deal of help for his Ṛig-Veda which is of immensely less value to South India than the Tiruvāçagam." He had a kindly appreciation of the Religion of the Tamiḻ people. He strongly repudiated the conduct of those who would thoughtlessly style us 'heathens' and unbelievers. He wrote to me to say, 'I am very much in agreement with what you write; but I cannot endure either the Theosophists or the Buddhists. The doctrine of 'Grace' expounded in the Siddhānta books was the thing that first attracted me to the system." He was a real lover of the Tamiḻ people and had expressed the most kindly sentiment towards them and appreciated their loyalty. He wrote in his 'Poets of the Tamiḻ lands' thus:—

"But the Tamiḻ race preserves most of its old virtues and has the promise of a noble future. Their English friends in teaching them all that the West has to impart, will find little to unteach in the moral lesson of the Kuṟaḷ rightly understood."

Again,

"This gnomic poetry has had a vast influence upon Tamiḻ character and possesses it still. There is no doubt in many respects the Tamiḻ people are among the foremost in the British Empire. Wherever Englishmen are found, these make their way. There is no Indian dialect a knowledge of which will carry a man further than the Tamiḻ. Tamiḻ Soldiers were with Clive in Arcot, with Coote at Porto novo, with Forde at Masulipatam, and in fact wherever a good fight had to be fought. We believe that Tamil ethical poetry has tended very much to fashion Tamil character."

"It is therefore to be desired that in Schools and Colleges the Study of Classical Tamil should be maintained. These quatrains are a well of good, old, strong, wholesome Tamil. They are calculated to strengthen and invigorate the character of the people. It is never good for a race to forget its old genuine literature." And yet our 'alma mater' would seem to have forgotten the value of this 'wholesome' Tamil* and our Government would not believe very much in our Tamil sepoys, who gave the rice to the

---

* And yet His Excellency Sir Arthur Havelock sounded the note of warning only a few years ago.

"To begin with such a measure obviously tends to reduce the temptation which exists to treat these Examinations mainly if not solely as qualifying for a Government or other employment; but apart from this, the consideration whether or not the Vernacular forms a more effective medium of education than the English Language, gives a strong additional ground for suggesting a careful examination of the desirability of change on its own merits. Does not learning in a foreign tongue cause waste of energy in the pupil and does it not impair accuracy of the knowledge acquired? Incidentally, too, such a measure is calculated to facilitate and stimulate in the higher educational grades, the study of the classical and vernacular literature of India. The strongest advocacy which I can suggest for this line of study is contained in the words of that illustrious statesman, Mounstuart Elphinstone, who writing in 1824 said, 'It would surely be a preposterous way of adding to the intellectual treasures of the languages to begin by the destruction of the indigenous literature, and I cannot but think that the future attainments of the natives will be increased in extent as well as in variety by being, as it were, engrafted on their own previous knowledge and imbued with their own original and peculiar character.' So much for the examination mania. There are other circumstances which obstruct completely sound educational policy in India. First, the immaturity of the Indian minds for the reception and assimilation of much Western teaching. No system of education is possible that does not teach Western ideas—social and political—and yet such ideas suddenly introduced among an alien

English Soldiers, drinking the '*Conjee*' themselves. Even as I write my eyes begin to water. And yet they talk of unrest and of the want of moral instruction in public schools. A moment's consideration would show how this want was supplied in the old schools. The whole system was a graduated system of wholesome ethical teaching. We commenced with the good old pial schools where nothing but moral text-books were taught. With baby lips we lisped 'அறஞ்செய விரும்பு' 'Love to do charity', 'ஆறுவதுசினம்' 'Put down anger', 'ஏற்பதிகழ்ச்சி' 'To beg is a disgrace', 'தந்தைதாய்ப் பேண்' 'Love and respect your parents', 'தீவினையகற்று' 'Rid yourself of evil', 'கண்டொன்றுசொல்லேல்', 'Don't tell lies', 'திருமாலுக்கடிமைசெய்' 'Worship God'. And the king was taught to be regarded as Parent, Guru and God. We began with 'ஆத்திசூடி,' 'Āttiçūdi', 'கொன்றைவேந்தன்' 'Konrai Vēndan', 'வெற்றிவேற்கை' 'Verri-Verkai' and finished in the pial schools with நீதிவெண்பா Nīti Venbā (meaning moral quatrains) and *Satakams* which taught the purely moral and homely duties. When we entered an English school, we had 'நல்வழி' 'Nalvaḷi' (meaning good path) and 'நன்னெறி' 'Nanneri' (meaning also the same), 'இனியவைநாற்பது' (Forty good things) and 'இன்னாநாற்பது' (Forty evil things), 'நீதிநெறி விளக்கம்' 'Light on the Moral Path', 'அறநெறிச்சாரம்' 'Essence of the Moral Path' and we finished with the Nālaḍi and the Kuraḷ in the college classes, supplemented by stories from Māhābhārata, Ramāyaṇa and Periapurāṇa. We challenge any language to possess such a graduated series of moral text-books as the Tamiḷ, and yet, which college is going to teach hereafter the Nālaḍi and the Kuraḷ? In my own

---

people, different from the West in religion, social and political habits and training, must at first produce an unhealthy condition. Much that is absorbed remains unassimilated, and undigested. Time is the only remedy for this, but much time will be needed. I am one of the many who feel strongly that no system of education can be sound unless religious teaching forms part of it. The difficulty of giving effect to this principle, I fear, is insuperable."

young days, there was a pial school in almost every street of Trichinopoly town. Most of the teachers were Paṇḍits, and my own teacher was a pensioned sepoy of stalwart proportions, and the moment he entered the school-room, all the babble would be hushed. He was a very strict disciplinarian. It was another pensioned sepoy who taught me English, after I had commenced it under my own beloved father. Where are all these schools gone? It is the Government Educational Department that has brought about their extinction. The Government Inspectors have brought out their new readers with sentences like 'குதிரை கனைக்கின்றது' 'Horse neighs' and 'நரி ஊளையிடுகின்றது' 'Jackal howls' and in the bigger readers learned articles on 'கரிவாயு' (carbonic acid gas) and 'Ali Baba and the Forty Robbers' find a place. All these might inform the young but it is all at the sacrifice of formation of character. I and my friends on the down grade of life have had reasons to regret the system of teaching pursued in the schools; and our children do not obey their parents nor their teachers, and when such respect for authority is lost at home and in the school, how can they have respect for their Sovereign Lord and King? The persons in charge of the village schools are mostly mere youths, who simply because they could not eke out the mere pittance in any other walk of life, take to this profession and they are ill-educated and half-learnt and with no moral backbone to enforce discipline. Why, my own little girl laughed at the mistake made by one of these so-called teachers. The extinction of these old indigenous and independent pial schools marks really the starting-point in the downward course in the moral teaching of South India. Even if we cannot resuscitate these old schools, a good start might be made by forming a committee to revise the studies and the text-books, from the lowest classes of schools, and to re-introduce the old text books as much as possible. The children at an early age can only learn by rote and imitation and it is absurd to force their intellect at this age and such attempts can only end in disaster. I wish the Tamiḻian Archæological Society will consider this question in all its aspects and make a suitable representation both to our University and Government at once.

In this digression, I have almost forgotten to say what was uppermost in my mind. I am afraid that the Tamiḻ people have not been altogether grateful to the late Rev. Dr. G. U. Pope. No doubt a subscription has been raised for a memorial in his name in connexion with the University, but many of the Subscribers were Europeans (all honour to them). I earnestly appeal however to all our Tamiḻ friends to subscribe at once to the Tablet to be erected in England and all subscriptions could be sent to Mr. J. V. Pope, Educational Advisor, Cochin State, Tiruchūr.

Going now to the consideration of the subject of Puṟaporuḷ dealt with in the following pages, one is landed really in an enquiry of a most interesting and vast nature. It is really an enquiry into the social, political, moral and intellectual condition of the ancient Tamiḻ people of more than 2000 years ago and of their civilization and their literature. This enquiry could occupy a book by itself and demand greater scholarship in Tamiḻ than I possess; but however, I will jot down what I may consider passing thoughts on the subject.

The first question that attracts our attention naturally is the length of time the Tamiḻ people had possessed their national literature and civilization in general and of the age of these two works in particular

With regard to the antiquity of the Tamiḻ nation and its ancient civilization, there is more or less a consensus of opinion among oriental scholars down to Prof. J. Vinson. The arguments on which they rest are all summed up by Mr. Senāthi Rājā in the last number of the 'Tamiḻian Antiquary' at pages 5, 6, and 7, namely, the direct trade with

South India in the days of king Solomon, the references in Vālmīki's Rāmāyaṇa to the Tamiḷ kingdoms, and in the Mahāvaṅšo, and in Ašoka's edicts, by Megasthenes, and Patañjali and by the Greek and Roman writers and travellers and by Varāhamihira and the Chinese travellers &c., and the ancient remains of Temples in the Java islands. To this, the Mahābhārata which is anterior to Gautama Buddha at least may be added. These carry the time to somewhere near 1000 B.C. These show that the Tamiḷ country possessed a settled kingdom, language and letters, a vast maritime trade &c. What is not admitted is that the Tamiḷs possessed a literature of their own before the 6th or 7th century A.D. Most of the European writers and some of our Indian friends too like the talented Mr. T. A. Gopinātha Rao would group almost all the famous Tamiḷ classics between the 6th and 7th centuries and 10th and 11th centuries A.D. And these few centuries would therefore seem to be a most remarkable period in the History of the Tamiḷ country and giving birth to all its literary treasures all at once. And we would have this curious fact also that the Tamiḷ people though possessing settled forms of Government and Arts &c., had not produced a single work worth mentioning for over a thousand years. Such literary barrenness cannot be thought of in the history of any nation. I am afraid they prove their case too much. Professor R. W. Frazer of the London University raised a laughter by remarking at the memorable meeting in honour of our Rev. Doctor as follows. "The grandest period of this literature fell somewhere between the ninth and the thirteenth centuries though to please their native friends they ought to place it 600 years earlier." It is not a question of pleasing us or not, but of historical accuracy; and it is not a mere matter of 600 years even as the Professor thinks. It is question of as many thousand years as Mr. S. A. Tirumalaikolundu Piḷḷai and the late Rai Bahadur C. W. Dāmodaram Piḷḷai have boldly put it. The world's civilization and art and letters did not begin with the Christian Era; and European savants now carry back Egyptian and Assyrian civilization several thousand years. Why should not South India which admittedly had considerable intercourse with the Phœnicians and Jews, Romans and Greeks and Arabians, have possessed as great an antiquity as these nations, and possessed a national literature of its own?

In any question, it will serve to reach truth if we can put away our prejudices and preconceived notions. Otherwise, no good will be gained by any enquiry. All that the few independent Tamiḻ Scholars crave for, is an open enquiry without favour or prejudice. In this enquiry, the value of the Tamiḻ literary records themselves are ignored though the Buddhist books containing the most exaggerated legends are taken more seriously. The entire tradition of the Tamiḻ people are set at nought. The Tamiḻ writers possessed a sense of truth and critical acumen remarkable in any country or nation, and yet they are credited with writing down so many packs of lies. In fact the record we possess of the Three famous Tamiḻ Sangams is a mere myth and not even the last Sangam or academy ever existed! However, to begin with, I take the general conclusions arrived at by the late Professor Sundaram Piḷḷai as regards the relative ages of the different classical works and as regards the upper limit of St. Jñānasambandha's age to be correct. Nobody has seriously assailed his conclusions and the main fact is supported by the weighty opinions of Rao Bahadur M. Venkayya and Dr. Hultzsch. He left the question of St. Māṇikkavāçaka's time in doubt and this was tackled by Mr. Tirumalaikoḷuṇdu and since handled by Messrs. T. A. Gopinātha Rao, T. Ponnambalam Piḷḷai and K. G. Seshayyar. Still, I am not convinced and I am prepared to leave it open still, though the balance of probabilities would seem to be in favour of the priority of the author of the Tiruvāçakam and the Tirukôvaiyār. As regards the existence of the Tamiḻ Academies, I agree mostly with the conclusions of Mr. Tirumalaikoḻuṇḍu Piḷḷai. There is ample testimony to the existence of such Tamiḻ Saṅgams. Mr. Tirumalaikoḻuṇḍu could have added the references to the Tamiḻ Saṅgam in St. Appar's hymns also. He tried to group most of the Poets of the Third Academy round the Pāṇḍiyan king Nedum C'eḻian, and C'eran king Seṅkuṭṭuvan, and C'oḻan king Karikālan. Mr. T. A. Gopinātha Rao attempts a similar grouping but would most unaccountably take it to the 6th and 7th centuries, postdating it even to the age of St. Jñānasambandha and St. Appar. One fact determines this question however. And this fact is admitted by Professor Śeshagiri Śāstriar, whom we know to be a most honest critic and a great scholar, unmeriting the serious denunciations of Mr. S. A. Tirumalaikoḻuṇḍu Piḷḷai,—that Pāṇḍiyan Nedum C'eḻian and Céran Seṅkuṭṭuvan were the contemporaries of the Gajavāhu I, whose age is fixed at 113 A.D. This would fix the age of the Third Saṅgam or academy and most of the classical works associated with this period including Puṟanāṉūṟu we are considering, as also that of the Sacred 'Kuṟaḷ'. The age of Puṟaporuḷ Veṇbā Mālai is possibly anterior, as it follows closely Tolkāppiyam and the lost work Panniru Paḍalam. The works of this period refer to the existence of the previous academies at *Ten Madurai* and *Kapāḍapuram* submerged by the sea. That this submergence was a fact seems to be well attested by science.* That this famous Kapāḍapuram is not a myth is proved from references in Vālmīki's Rāmāyaṇam itself. The learned editor of *Sen Tamiḻ* discusses this question in No. 3, Vol. VII of this most useful monthly, the organ of the Fourth Tamiḻ Saṅgam founded by that large-hearted nobleman Śrīmān P. Pāṇḍithuraisāmi Devar Avergaḷ. The extract from

* See the point discussed by Paṇḍit D. Savariroyan at p. 198, Vol. X, 'Light of Truth' or 'The Siddhānta Dīpika' and elsewhere.

Rāmāyaṇa is to this effect: "Filled with gold, and possessed of beauty, and adorned with pearls, you will see the *Kapāḍa* dear to the Pāṇḍiyans." The editor points out how the northern commentators bungled over this passage and interpreted *Kapāḍa* as a gate but that Govindarājā interpreted it correctly as the city of Kapāḍapura. Whatever the truth about the Rāmāyaṇa story may be, the book and the author thereof are no myths. Vālmīki also makes mention of the Town of *Murasipaṭṭaṇam* on the west coast which could be no other than *Musiripaṭṭaṇam* which continued down to the day of the Latin voyagers. The first Saṅgam was said to have been presided over by Agastya, and that there was one who bore the name of Agastya in the South even before the time of Vālmīki there can be no doubt, and there are his literary remains preserved in the commentaries on the ancient works. Among the poets of the first academy is found the name of one Vāḷmīki. One Tamiḻ piece by him is contained in the Puṟanāṉūṟu. The author of 'Vālmīki' was a hunter by caste, Veda or Veḍḍah, and these Veḍḍahs are found from Viṇdhya to Ceylon and they were a Tamiḻ tribe and traces of Tamiḻ and Tamiḻ tribes are found all through India and up to Beluchistan. Could it be that the Poet of Rāmāyaṇa was also a Tamiḻian and that after he became famous was admitted into the Tamiḻ Academy? We find such names as Gotamanār (Gautama) and Kapilar (Kapila) among Tamiḻ poets who were at the same time great sages and Sanskritists. If according to the Sanskrit and Tamiḻ accounts, Tamiḻ kings took part in the great Mahābhārata War, why should not Sanskrit Paṇḍits and Sages have travelled to the South and been honoured by the Tamiḻ Academicians? The account of the first two Academies contains long lists of kings. That at least one name in the first list is not apocryphal is now proved. In the Annual Report of the Assistant Archæological Superintendent for Epigraphy for the year 1907-1908, the Veḷvikuḍi Śāsanam is published, and it refers to two ancient Pāṇḍiyan Kings Palyāga Mudu

Kuḍumi Peru Vaḷuthi and Kaḍuṅkôn. This Peruvaḷuthi is admitted to be a remote ancestor of Neḍum C'eḷiyan of Talayalaṅkam fame, whom we traced to the first century. The poets who sang of him, Kārikiḷar Nettimaiyār and Neḍumpaḷḷiattanār naturally do not figure in the lists of the Third Academy. The *Kaḍuṅkôn* of the inscription is taken by Mr. T. A. Gopinātha Rao to be the last of the kings of the Third Academy as given in the preface of Iṟaiyanār-Agapporuḷ (vide his article in No. 10 Vol. VI. of *Sen Tamiḷ*). That this is a mistake is pointed out by P. G. in No 12 Vol. VI. of the same. This Preface speaks of Kaḍuṅkôn not as the last of the 3rd Academy but as the last of the First Academy. As P. G. points out, the attempt of Mr. Gopinātha Rao to bring down the dates of Peruvaḷuthi and Neḍumçeḷian to the 6th and 7th centuries is inconsistent with other proved facts, such as the age of Jñānasambandha. If the age of Neḍumçelian is taken to be the first century after Christ, then the time of Peruvaḷuthi and Kaḍuṅkôn should precede it by several centuries, and this would really approximate it to the age of Rāmāyaṇa and Mahābhāratā and the first and second academies. We would leave the discussion here for the present and touch upon other points connected with the subject of Puṟaporuḷ Veṇbā Mālai and Puṟa-nānūṟu, taking it as proved that these works are not later than the first century A.C., though the Puṟa-nānūṟu might contain pieces of far greater antiquity.

Turning to the condition of Society prevailing at the time, it will be noted that Puṟaporuḷ Veṇbā Mālai follows the divisions of Society already set forth in the Tolkāppiyam (Poruḷ, Sūtras 75 and 626 *et seq*). The people are divided into Arasar (Kshatriyas), Antaṇar or Pārpār (Brāḥmans), Vāṇikan or Vaiśikan (Vaiśyas), and Veḷān (Veḷḷāḷahs). It will be noted that the term Sūdra is nowhere used. Under Sūtra 75, Vāṇikan and Veḷān are classed together, and six functions are allotted to them. The commentators state what these six functions are: Reciting the Vedas, Performing Yagjñas, Making gifts, Cultivation, Tending cattle and Trading. In the edition published by Mr. Dāmodaram Piḷḷai,* the commentator would restrict in the case of Veḷān the 'Reciting' to reciting of books other than the Vedas and would substitute *Vaḻipāḍu*' 'service' for '*Veḷḷāḷahs*', and he also notices the views of others who make no such distinction, but who would divide them into a higher and lower class and would opine that service should be ascribed to the lower class only. Nachchinārkiniar in his commentary on '*Marabial*' shows that Veḷḷāḷahs could give their girls in marriage to those of the kingly class and could serve in the army as commanders and could become kings of the second class and be called '*Arasu*' and *Vēḷ*. (Kurunilamannar). Vide Vol. II, No. 11, p. 366, *Sen Tamiḻ*. It may be noticed that Śrī Kṛishṇa himself did not belong to the highest kshatriya caste and was therefore looked down upon by other kings, though girls from Śrī Kṛishṇa's family were freely given in marriage to the real kshatriyas. Tolkāppiyar himself does not recognize any distinctions among the functions allotted to Vaiśyas and Veḷḷāḷahs. He however says in Sūtra 635 that though Veḷḷāḷahs have various functions, it is best to describe them as engaged in cultivation. Of course all these rules are for use in poetry and in speaking of a particular class, their chief functions and weapons, trade, implements, flowers worn &c., have to be mentioned. Possibly the mention of the lower castes is omitted because they are not fit subjects of poetry. The Puṟa-poruḷ (8. 11.) accordingly speaks of their *Vāgai* as excellence in cultivation, and their 'service' is no servility is clear from the other terms in the stanza and in their being described as the very 'Life of the World', 'உலகுக்குயிர்'.

* The editor of *Sen Tamiḻ* thinks that this commentary on *Marabial* published in the name of Nachchinārkiniar is not his and that the real author is Pērāsiriar, and he especially deals with the more liberal views of Nachchinārkiniar regarding Veḷḷāḷahs. (Vol. II. No. 11).

This phrase 'உலகுக்குயிர்' is also the very phrase used to describe the king in several pieces of Puṟa-nānūṟu also.

However the curious question arises who these Vêḷan or Veḷḷāḷars were and why they are described by this term and not by the term Sūdras, and if they formed the indigenous people of South India. Because it is well to remember that these distinctions we have till now considered were brought into use after the northern Āryans had settled in the country, and this settlement should have taken place at least 2000 or 3000 years before the Christian Era. Tolkāppiyam though written long after, is only important to us as containing glimpses of the earlier races that inhabited the country. This part of the subject is dealt with partly in Mr. Senāthirājah's paper and I may touch on it briefly. The country was divided into five திணைகள் (Tiṇai), Kuriñji (Hill country), Mullai (Forest), Marutham (Irrigated land), Neithal (Seaboard), and Pālai (desert); and the peoples inhabiting these tracts were respectively called Kuṟavar, Iḍayar, Uḻavar, Paṟavar and Maṟavar or Veḍar, and each had their chieftains called Kôn or *Mannavan*. Each had their peculiar occupations and marriage-customs as determined by their environments. For instance, where speaking of the Kuriñji Mâkkaḷ (people) poets speak of secret marriage (gāndharvam) and for Marutha Mâkkaḷ, marriage. Why should this be? When coming down from Šrī Šailam, I fell into conversation with a *Cheñchu* and asked him how they got married. He said, "Why, Sir, the boys and girls roam about these hills and they come together, and form ties, and when this is known to the parents, they publish this over a pot of toddy." I wrote as follows in my article on Šrī Parvatam (L. T. Vol. III. p. 217). "Just in the same way as we read of in Kuriñjipāṭṭu (one of the Ten Tamiḻ Idylls.*). Of course the environments favour them so much and the people are so few and the liberty of movement is so great that you cannot but

* A full summary of it is given by me in L. T. Vol. I. p. 16.

expect such marriages among such a community. Of course our poets and lawyers put it as though such and such a kind of marriage is required for such a kind of land (Tiṇai, திணை); and our friend Mr. T. Veerabadra Mudaliar wonders, why our poets should of necessity people 'Marutham' (மருதம்) with prostitutes and dancing girls. Of course, there is no necessity, but as in their view மருதம் (Marutham), the land covered with paddy-fields represented the seat of wealth and luxury, with civilized activity and prostitution following in their wake, the poets always lay down that wherever 'civilized towns' are spoken of, prostitution should also be mentioned." Marriage is the normal status of people living in villages and towns, and prostitution is a necessary evil of such restricted societies, which even the most highly advanced civilization of the 20th century has not been able to rid itself of. I used to puzzle Sanskrit pundits by asking why 'gāndharva' form is introduced in 'Śakuntala' and why the regular form in 'Mālati Mādhaviyam'. The Tamil Paṇḍit armed with his Tolkāppiyam would have had no difficulty in answering the question. The *Tiṇai* in Śakuntala is Kuriñji and the one in the latter work is 'Marutham', Township. Poruḷ Sūtra 14 gives the Poruḷ for the various *Tiṇai*. Such as secret union and all incidents connected therewith for *Kuriñji*, separation for *Pālai*, waiting for *Mullai*, pining for the absent lover for *Nèithal*, and sulking for *Marutham*. 'Neithal' is the sea-board; and the lovers go abroad on the bottom of ships in search of wealth and merchandise. The woman sits pining after her absent lord. Those who had seen the classic picture of the European artists depicting a woman seated on the open battlements of the fort near the sea-shore with her eyes strained over the expanse of the waters would better appreciate this *Neithal-Poruḷ*. There is a community among poets and artists of all climes and nations, and the secret is the Study of Nature which is uniform. The *Poruḷ* of Pālai is separation. The lover proposes a journey. The wife fears every danger at once to her husband and would not hear of the separation, and if need be, she proposes to share the danger with him. Why how many a time did my wife fear of an accident similar to the Kāramadai accident whenever I proposed a railway journey even though it was of a short distance. When the whole of Poruḷ-Adikāram is properly translated and annotated and understood by the European Literati, then alone will its importance to the world of Poetry be clearly appreciated. I give below the *Karu* கரு (environment) of the Kuriñji which will serve to illustrate the others also. They are "Food: a coarse Paddy, Millet and Bamboo rice; Animals; Tigers, Elephants, bears and boars; Trees: Agil, Sandal, Teak, *Timis*, and *Kino*; Birds: Parrots and peacocks; Musical instruments: *Murukiam* and Thondaka Drum; Occupation: securing honey and digging up edible roots, and cultivation of Millet and scaring away of Parrots from the millet-fields; Music: Kuriñjiyal; Flowers: Flowers of Kāndal, Veṅgai (Kino) and blue lotus; Water: Hill torrents and Pools; Village: Sirukuḍi, Kurichchi. This is the grammar of 'Ahapporuḷ'. The same applies to Puṟa-poruḷ' also. There is a correspondence between the Tiṇai divisions in 'Aham' and the divisions in 'Poruḷ'. Kuriñji corresponds to '*Vetchi*' and the scene of the latter is accordingly a hill fortress. *Vañji* corresponds to *Mullai*; uliñai to 'Marutham', *Tumbai* to '*Neithal*'; Vāgai to *Pālai*; Kañji to Peruṇthiṇai; Kaikiḷai to Pādān; and all these are necessary to understand the structure of the different Paḍalams in Puṟa-poruḷ Veṇbā Mālai; and it is not understanding the grammar of 'Puṟam' as set forth in Tolkāppiyam that makes Dr. Pope remark that some of the pieces in the later Paḍalams are misplaced. 'Puṟam' does not comprise merely war as stated by Mr. Senāthi Rāja, but comprises all the activities of human society not comprised by 'Aham' or Pure Love; and in what department of human activity does not love enter? You have to describe the love and woes of the bereaved mother or wife in connection with war as in peace. Puṟam in fact corresponds to the first two Parts of the Sacred 'Kuraḷ,' 'Aṟam,' and 'Poruḷ' or 'Dharma' and 'Artha', and the generic word Poruḷ in Ahapporuḷ and Puṟa-poruḷ corresponds to the word *artha* in Purushārtha. And the Purushārtha is four: 'Aṟam', 'Poruḷ', 'Inbam', 'Veeḍu', or Dharma, Artha, Kāma and Moksha. And Toḷkāppiyam is the grammar of the first three Purushārthas, and no such grammar do we possess in any other language of the world.

We began with a disquisition about the castes and ended most inconsequently enough with the whole subject-matter of 'Aham' and 'Puṟam'. The main question has to be considered yet. If the *Marutha Mākkaḷ* were the Paḷḷars and Parayahs as Paṇḍit Savariroyan thinks, how is their present down-fallen condition to be accounted for. I for one do not see much light so far and must leave it for further investigation. The position of Vēḷan or Veḷḷāḷah is also a curious one. I have noticed the high position they [the Veḷḷāḷahs] occupy in Tolkāppiyam. But who are they and how they came into the land are questions requiring much investigation. The Vēḷ is defined in Pinkalaṇdai Nigaṇḍu as meaning God Muruga, (Subramaṇya) Manmatha (God of love) and king of the chalukyas. In the Telugu language, the term Vēlpu which we fancy should be traced to the same root, means Deva or God generally. Among the Telugus also there is a class called Velamas. In a couple of interesting papers published by the Editor of the *Sen Tamiḷ* (Vide No. 2 Vol. 8) he identifies the 'Vēḷir' mentioned in the Tamiḷ classics as dwellers of the Āṇdra country and with the chalukyas and Hoisala Vellāḷahs, and their country 'Vēl pulam' or Vēnāḍ as portion of the present Bombay presidency comprising the districts of Belgaum and Sholapur; and he thinks also that these were originally Tamiḷ settlements. It is matter for further investigation whether Vēḷān or Vellāḷahs came from the West and supplanted the original cultivators of the soil, namely the Pallars. It is also to be remembered that the Pandia country was actually over-run by a Foreign Prince from the West called *Kalapravarasan* after the time of Peruvaḷuthi as set forth in the *Vêḷur* grant already referred to, and this Foreign prince is identified with a Kanarese King by both Messrs. Veṇkayya and Gopinatha Rao. I have indicated all these to show in what directions further investigations should advance.

Regarding the art of Government, as evidenced in the Puṟapporuḷ Veṇba Mālai and Puṟa-nānūru, it is seen to be in the most advanced form. They had a regular army, with cavalry and elephant corps. They had bows and arrows and spears and swords. They knew the different ways of fighting an enemy by siege and in the open battle-field. They had spies. They had well-constructed fortresses and towns surrounded by deep moats and a line of forest. They had very brave soldiers; and the few pieces translated by Dr. Pope and by myself bear ample testimony to this. Though in their rage they are implacable, yet no one ventured into a war unless forced by sheer necessity and without deeply considering all the horrors of war. The first event is the capturing of the enemy's cattle. Whatever its origin in even much remoter times, this act is put down as an act of charity so as to remove these useful and sacred animals from the scene of War. The invader was equally humane to the aged and infirm and the childless, and women and Brahmans.

They had a very high ideal of Kingship. His prowess in war, his immutable justice and accessibility, his protecting hand over the poor, and his liberality and piety are all set forth. Though the Glory of the King is a strong army, yet virtue is his chief strength. With strength like that of the sun, and grace like that of the moon, and charity like that of the rain, his days could be counted like the sands in front of the great Sendil of God Muruga (P.N.N. 55). He should guide his people and the affairs of state as one guides a car on a proper road. (185). His umbrella should protect the oppressed. The triumph of the king is the result of the produce of the soil raised from the sweat of the cultivator. When there is drought and dearth, and people become wicked, the world will blame the King. Without listening to lying counsel, when cultivators are protected and through them other people also, then will the king merit the praise of even his enemies. When the king grants his great love and peace to his people, his people feel for his safety as for themselves. The king is the life of his people.

நெல்லுமுயிரன்றே நீருமுயிரன்றே
மன்னனுயிர்த்தே மலர்தலையுலகம்
அதனால், யானுயிரென்பதறிகை
வேன்மிகுதானைவேந்தர்க்குக் கடனே.

Food stuff is not the life nor water ;
The king is the life of the world.
Therefore to know he is the life,
Is the duty of the king with a large army. (186)

A beautiful simile is given to illustrate how the king should collect the taxes. The produce of even a small field would last for many days, if used in little handfuls. 100 acres overrun by a mad elephant would not last even a day (184). At the same time obedience to the king and fervent loyalty to him is inculcated. He is their very life. He is their God, and Rajadroham (Treachery to the King) is one of the worst sins a man can be guilty of. While on this question I would draw the attention of the reader to the series of papers published in 'Sen Tamil' (Nos. 1 to 3, Vol. VIII) from the pen of that talented Mahomedan gentleman and poet, M. K. M. Abdul Kader Rowther, on 'இந்தியா இறைமாட்சி' 'Indian Kingship', which article should be translated into English and published and distributed free to every student in Schools and Colleges. While we have portrayed the ancient ideal of a king, how blessed we feel when in the person of His Majesty, Our

Sovereign Lord and King, Emperor Edward VII, we realise all this ideal.

Pura-poruḷ Veṇbā Mālai VIII. 19 shows that the king had also his council of elders and their qualifications are also mentioned. It is as follows:

"The council (அவைக்களம்) should possess the eight qualities and should always look to success after duly weighing chances of victory and defeat, after debating justly the questions raised and the objections urged."

The eight qualities are stated to be good birth, learning, good character, Truthfulness, Purity, ornament of even-mindedness, without being envious and being covetous; and they are ideal characteristics which if possessed would bring glory to the land. There was an additional safeguard to the wayward actions of the king, in the class of Poets who were the sages and wise men of those days. They were the privileged class as Dr. Pope observes, and they tendered their good counsel without fear or favour and the king dared not injure them, as their person was considered sacred.

With regard to the arts and industries, they possessed all the fine arts including music, painting and sculpture. The references to the Vīrakal put up in honor of the departed heroes, has many a point to illustrate. This is found in Tolkāppiyam itself. It shows that so far back, people knew how to sculpture in stone. If so, they could build palaces and Temples and fortresses in stone. This has to be carried at least a thousand year before Christ. If so, the theory of the famous archæologist James Fergusson has to be revised considerably. In his view, the Buddhists were the first to construct caves and stupas &c., in stone. They began with the simplest structures, and the style became more ornate afterwards. It was from the Buddhist, the Hindus began to learn the art of building in stone, (forgetting that Buddhists themselves were Hindus) and the Brahminical Temples were of later origin and, but from the fact that actual inscriptions are found in the Hindu Cave Temples of Badami &c., dated 6th century A.D., he would have taken the age of Hindu Temples to a much later period. The Puṟanāṉūṟu speaks of Temples dedicated to Śiva (P.N.N. 6) and to God Muruga (55) at Tiruchendur in the Tinnevelly District. Was the structure built on the sands at the latter place one of wood, if Mr. Fergusson's theory be true? We might as well fancy a temple built of sand! The very earliest record of Madura is its centrally situated temple and its famous Indra Vimāna. The only exception among Indian Temples is the famous shrine at Chidambaram which is of wood (the central portion). But this probably carries the antiquity of the Temple (கோயில்) several thousand years back. In the first century A.D., there were innumerable Hindu Temples all over the land, of great magnificence and splendour, and scattered here and there were also Buddhist shrines and chaityas and *Topes*. The word Tope is a corruption of the word stupa or stupi which is a crowning part of the Hindu Temple and the Kumbābhishegam ceremonies are connected with the consecrating of this. Instead of the Brahmans borrowing from the Buddhists their Temple architecture, it is the latter that have borrowed from the Hindus. When they first began, they were a small community and poor, and their buildings were simple. But when they grew in power and affluence, richer shrines followed. It could also be noticed that Buddhists have actually made use of the older Hindu Temples and altered it or added to it. Of course, so far as the art is concerned, it is absurd to talk of the Buddhist or the Hindus copying art from each other, as they were all Hindus. According to Mr. Fergusson there are no earlier structures than those built in king Asoka's time; but without the art already in existence for several centuries before him, he could not have evolved all in a moment and flooded the country with his Topes and Pillars. While feeling extremely grateful to those Europeans who have done valuable service in this department, I feel sure that greater light would be thrown on these questions if Indians would take to the study of the subject with the same ardour which European scholars have displayed. The other point of importance connected with the Vīrakal is the circumstance that letters were inscribed on these stones setting forth their names and great deeds. Nearly a whole section in chapter X. I. (P.V.M.) is devoted to it (Verses 7 to 14). Verse 12 is what refers to the inscribing of the hero's name in the stone image. This is indicated in sutra 60 of Poruḷ, Tolkāppiyam. In 264 (P.N.N.) this inscribing the name (பெயர் பொறித்தல்) is also expressly referred to. So that it is clear that before the first century A.D., Tamiḻ had a written script. When we note that from and before the age of Tolkāppiyam, the letters were called 'எழுத்து' 'eḻuttu' 'meaning what is written', the possession of the written script should be traced at least a thousand years back. Paṭṭinapālai (one of the Ten Idylls in praise of Karikāla of the first century A.D., refers to the goods heaped up in the custom house and the bags being marked with the mark of the Tiger (King C'ola's sign) &c. When we take all these with the fact that with the Vatteḻuttu, we have a unique indigenous script unconnected with any other script*, we may fairly lay claim to possessing one of the oldest scripts of the world.

Dr. A. C. Burnell is good enough to prove at p. 132, (Elements South Indian Paleography) that South India is the source of the early civilization of Java and that the Kawi and hence the modern Javanese alphabets came from W. Java or Pallava Type. He admits that the Tamilian alphabet is not derived from the Sanskrit and its phonetic system has remained so from its origin, and it has not changed since 3rd century B.C.

* 'The amount of proof that the Vatteluttu is of independent origin, and not derived from the S. Asoca character, appears to be conclusive." p. 130. '*Elements of S. I. Paleography*'.

He admits that the Vatteḷuttu is independent of other scripts, and yet he says (p. 127) it is impossible to put the introduction of writing at so early a date (3rd century B.C.) There is no inherent impossibility in the thing, except prejudice. And the absence of rare inscriptions can be no proof that such script was not in existence at a much anterior time. There is however a remark of his at the head of the same page which, if correct, could prove my case far better. It is this: "The omission of the Tamiḷ grammarians to notice the fact that the consonants have double values (viz., as surds and sonants) is unaccountable except that they had to deal with a language already reduced to writing." As I had stated, writing was already in existence when Tolkappiyam came to be written and all that we have to do is to determine the age of Tolkappiyam. According to Nachchinarkiniar, Tolkappiyam was composed before even Veda Vyāsa arranged the Vedas into Ṛig, Yajur, Sāman and Atharvaṇa. It is at any rate anterior to Pāṇini, as there is no reference to it in Tolkāppiyam but to *aindram*, the very first Sanskṛit work on grammar like Agathiyam, now extinct.

That the art of painting was also practised from an early time is evident. (P.N.N. 251). The way in which every Temple is covered with frescoes in colour should show their great love of the art.

That the people delighted in music and dancing, both men and women, and they had various musical instruments like குழல், யாழ், கின்னரி, முழா, &c., is also evident from these pages. (See in particular last two verses of last chapter P.V.M.) That the Tamiḷs were a joyous people and led luxurious lives is also clear. They adorned themselves with ornaments and fine muslins * and sandal-paste and their

* See piece translated from Kalittogai. p. 186, Vol. III, S. D. Mr. Fergusson remarks that the Indian sculptures appear almost nude: but this is not from want of clothing. The artist wanted to show as in the cases quoted above that the muslin did not conceal the body.—J. M. N.

love of flowers was inordinate†. They had a language of flowers in love and another in war, so much so that even Vālmīki has remarked on it. § They were fond of food and drink, and toddy was their chief drink till they learnt to quaff off golden goblets, the sweet wine brought by the Romans or Greeks (Yavaṉar). (Vide P. N. N. 56.)

Their trade was vast and their industries many. We must go to the description in Pattinappālai to gauge the extent of their trade. India was then the centre of the world even as it is now, the meeting place of the various nations and religions of the world. They knew the art of boat and ship-building and weaving and dyeing and working in gold and metals. They had early attained to the highest proficiency in the art of agriculture and irrigation; and we have it in the Mahavanso that as early as the 6th century B.C., the Ceylonese borrowed the art from the Tamiḻs. One piece from Purananūru is translated by Dr. Pope, No. 18, in which the poet Kuḍaviyalanār advises the King to increase irrigation-works; and that most indefatigable worker for the good of India, I mean Sir F. Nicholson, when I showed the piece to him, was most delighted with it.

Among the amusements, besides the driving of horses yoked to a single car, and of elephants &c., they indulged in cock-fighting and partridge-fighting and sheep-fighting. They had regular target practice. Gambling was not unknown. I will finish my introduction with noticing the religion of the times. As set forth in Sutra 5 (Poruḷ, Tolkāppiyam) the people of the different Tiṇai (திணை) had different deities. The pastoral tribes worshipped Vishṇu; The Hill tribes worshipped God Muruga or Subramaṇya; The Paravas worshipped God Varuṇa, and the *Marutha*

† Even now, no people in India spend so much on flowers for feasts and festivals as the people of the South.

§ See 'Sen Tamiḻ' Vol. 8. No. 1.

Makkal worshipped God Indra. The question is raised by Dr. Pope and others whether God Muruga was not a South Indian God unconnected with the later Hinduism. He might or might not have been, but whereas we see the other tribal divinities are also deities of the Hindu Pantheon, to exclude one alone, does not seem to be warranted by any authority. The Koyas, the Hill tribe of the Godavery agency have for the symbol of their God, a spear or Trident which they call *Vêlpu*, and they indulge in a curious dance dressed in bullock's horns and peacock-feathers; but whether they have any idea of God Muruga, I have not been able to ascertain. And by the way, the dance in honor of God Muruga is spoken of as a devil-dance by Dr. Pope, but I am not sure if this is the best way of describing it. There are dances in honour of every Divinity, and the highest Brahmins of the land dance before God Natarājah in Chidambaram, when he grants his Darsan on Arūdra day. Dance has always been described as the music of motion and expresses the highest emotion of mankind of every shade. No doubt, the dance in honor of God Muruga was also accompanied by animal sacrifice. And animal sacrifice was from the beginning connected with the earliest Aryan observance. God Muruga is no doubt spoken of everywhere in the Tamil classics as the son of Siva, but we have no authority for Dr. Pope's identification of Him as the son of Korravai or Durga. That this latter deity is satisfied with gory sacrifices and is invoked by the warrior host is also evidenced by the Mahābhārata. In the Durgastava, there she is no doubt identified with Pārvati, and the Sakti-worship prevailing in North India, would seem to be consistent with it. But it is a remarkable fact connected with the worship of Ṣiva and Pārvati in the South that it is perfectly pure and holy and uncontaminated by any bloody sacrifice. At the Temple of Brahmaramba in Ṣri Sailam, there is animal sacrifice offered, but as I have noted elsewhere, this temple is situated outside the square of the temple of God Ṣiva and

Pārvati and the officiating priest is a Smārta and not a Tamballā (Tabopala) as is the priest of the Śiva shrine. In Kanchipuram also, the Temples of Kāmātchi and Śiva are outside each other and are presided over by Smārta and Gurukal priests respectively. And besides this, we find actually a Temple of *Koṟṟavai* or Durga, on the outer skirts of the village only, at the gateway of cities and towns, though in the centre there is a great Śiva shrine and that of Pārvati* All these show that this abomination is not indigenous to South India but one transplanted from the north.†

Then is another remark of Dr. Pope which we take exception to and which is not correct. Talking of Puṟa-nānūṟu he says (see p. 4.) 'It is worthy of note, also, that of these poems except the introductory invocation (which is of later date by Perun Tevanār, the translator of Mahā Bhāratam) none make any decided allusion to Śiva-worship'. On the other hand the allusions are only too numerous. (See the references given in the index of subject-matter (விசேடகுறிப்புகள்,) in Mahā Mahopādhyaya Swāminātha Iyer's edition under the word 'Śivaperumān'. One most significant piece is No. 6 in this collection. In this, the king is advised to cover his umbrella in front of the Temple of the Three-eyed Śiva, praised by the Munis of the Four Vedas. This is addressed by Kāri Kiḻār to Pāṇḍiyan Palyāgasālai Mudukuḍumi Peruvāḷuthi, who is the first in the Velur grant; and it shows that the Temple of God Śiva was in the middle of the Town, as now in Madura, and the God was worshipped by the Highest castes.§ Even in *Maṇimékalai*, the most respectful

* Dr. Burnell is certainly wrong when he says that the great Hindu Temple is not in the centre of the towns. He is evidently carried away by the example of Tanjore Temple, which it may be noted is not an old Temple but quite a modern one finding no place in the Devāra Hymns.

† See my article 'What is Kali' in p. 13, Vol. III. S. D.

§ See Muir's Texts, Vol. IV, where Lassen is quoted to show that in the Mahābhārata, Śiva is the God of the Higher castes.

mention of Šiva is made. He is the deity invoked in Tolkāppiyam and all other ancient classics. In Puṟap-poruḷ Veṇbā Māḷai, there is this quatrain by Ayyanārithanār himself.

> "Let our eyes see him. Our ears hear His praise.
> Let our mouth utter songs in his honour and our legs walk round Him.
> Him who stands like the Ghee (in milk) in countless lives
> Him with the Blue Throat, let my palms lift up in worship."

Mr. James Fergusson frequently says that the worship of Šiva was the most ancient and that Vaishṇavism was a degenerate form of Buddhism,* and this he does from his

* "Šiva is and apparently as far as our information goes, seems always to have been, the favourite deity in the South, and his name and that of his consort is mixed with so many legends, and these extend so far back, that it almost looks as if his worship sprung up there. On the other hand, the earliest authentic mention of Siva is by a Greek author, Bardanes, who describes him in a cave not far from Peshawar in the early part of the 3rd century under the well-known form of Ardhanāri, or half-man and half-woman. He is also found unmistakably in the coins of Kadphises with his trident and bull, before the Christian Era, and it is not clear whether these are fragments of mythology left there by the Dravidians dropped like the Brahmi language on their way to India, or whether it is a local northern cult which the Brahmans brought with them to India, and finally transported into the South."

"Though the worship of Vishṇu is as fashionable and nearly as extensively prevalent in modern times, in the South, as that of Šiva, it certainly never arose among the Dravidian races. It is essentially a cultus that could only have had its origin among the same people as those from whom the Buddhist religion first took its present form. It is in fact at the present day only a very corrupt form of that religion so corrupt, indeed, that their common origin is hardly to be recognised in its new disguise, but still undoubtedly springing from a cognate source though very far from emulating either the virtue or the purity of its elder-sister-faith. Borrowing apparently a cosmogony from Assyria, Vishnuvism separated from Buddhism, attracting to itself most of the study of the thousands of Šaivite Temples scattered throughout the length and breadth of India. This furnishes in a way a disproof of the theory of some people, both friends and enemies, who say that Šiva worship was indigenous to South India. The more I study the records both in Tamil and Sanskrit, the more am I convinced that this theory cannot be maintained, and the personality we now possess of Siva is fully borne out by the picture in Rig Veda itself.

J. M. NALLASWAMI.

RAJAHMUNDRY,
1, Chitrai, 1910.

---

local superstitions that had crept into that religion, and finally becoming fused by the all-powerful solvent of the Vedas, it forms a powerful element in the Modern Brahminical religion as now existing in India." —'Cave Temples of India,' pp. 20 and 21. I do not share in these views of Dr. Furgusson on the origin of Vaishṇavism. In P. V. M. his worship is frequently mentioned, and several stories of Šri Krishṇa find mention in the Tamil classics which are not recorded in the Sanskrit Purāṇas and Itihāsas, thus proving their great antiquity. (Vide No. 1 Vol. *Sen Tamil*).

P.S.—After I had sent this paper to the press, Srimath M. Ragava Iyengar, the learned editor of 'Sen Tamiḻ' was good enough to send his paper on 'Velir', and our doubts are even more than justified in regard to the position of Vellāḷahs. And the solution which he offers seems very highly probable. His position is that these were of the race of Śri Krishṇa himself and were Kshatriyas; and that after the fall of Dvāraka these spread themselves into the South and colonised the Bombay Presidency, and the Tamiḻ lands, and were soldiers, cultivators and merchants and tenders of cattle, and engaged themselves in other industrial occupations like house-building etc. The cultivators occupied '*marutham*'; and the shepherds occupied the '*mullai*', and owing to the nature of their occupation became less civilized*, came to be called *Āyar* or shepherds, and they held in special honour Vishṇu and his incarnation Śrī Kṛishṇa. The cultivators came to call themselves Vellāḷahs, and their special occupation was therefore called *Veḷḷāṇmai*; and they became divided into a lower and higher order,—the cultivators who tilled their own lands, and those who got their lands tilled by others. From the upper class * came also the soldiers, generals, officers of state, and minor kings called குறுநிலமன்னர். With these families, the great kings also allied themselves †. The great Vél Pāri

---

* In some of the mofussil stations I have been, several members of the same family had to appear before me as witnesses. Of these, one attended to the business of the family and was intelligent. One or two attended to cultivation, and one attended solely to tending cattle; and his intelligence was of the lowest order, hardly differing from that of the animals he tended through life, exhibiting the law of reflection and assimilation as set forth by Professor Henry Drummond in his famous address, a 'Changed Life.'

* The high officers of State were dignified with the title of 'Mudaliar' as I have observed elsewhere. They formed the household personal attendants on the great kings and were called hence 'Ahamudayar.' Those of them that stuck to pure trade were called *Veḷān* chetty.

† The Veḷḷāḷas call themselves 'Piḷḷai' and *Piḷḷaimār*, meaning 'son;' and could it be they were titled so, as they were sons of kings by such alliance?

of immortal fame and other great *Vallals* were of this class and were noted for their liberality, and the term Vêl became synonymous with 'liberality' and 'king'. The portion of Bombay Presidency above Konkan was called Veṇāḍu (Vêl Nāḍu) and is mentioned in Tamiḷ works and *Koduṇ* Tamiḷ nāḍu. If these investigations stand the test of further scrutiny, they ought to be of the greatest importance to the progress of our Tamiḷ people. They ought to tend towards the abolition of all distinctions between *piḷḷais* and Mudaliars, and Vêlan Chetties and *Ahamuḍayars*. The food question would stand in the way to some extent, but it has to be remembered that no such distinction was observed even as between Brāhmans and non-brāhmans once.

One other point I wish to notice regarding the *Tāli* of the Tamiḷs. The Tamiḷ people and all Tamil Brāhmins of the South, wear a curiously shaped *Tāli* with their māṅgalya sūtram. The Telugus wear a *Boṭṭu*. The shape of the Tamilian's Tāli had excited my curiosity for a long time. The Brāhmin Paṇḍit whom I consulted could give me no solution and could quote no authorities for the preparation and wearing of this Tāli. Paṇḍit Mākaral Kārthikeya Mudaliar told me however that the shape was that of a Tiger's Molar tooth, and gave me a reference in 'Tirukôvaiyār' in which it is spoken of as புலிப்பற்றலி 'Pulippaṟṟāli.' The mention of this Tāli made of a tiger's tooth is found in P.N.N. also, No. 374. This is highly suggestive. We have to go back to a period when brides were won by prowess shown in killing a tiger and the tiger's tooth was tied in consequence. After a time, it was made in gold and tied; and this is probably one of the very many customs adopted by the Brahmins. The Telugu word for Tāli is the same. In my childhood I wore a neck-ornament with a pendent made of tiger's claws. Reference to this ornament is also found in the classics. Such things have gone out of fashion now.•

J. M. N.

"PUṞA-PORUḶ VEṆBĀ-MĀLAI".

PART I.

"PURA-PORUL VENBĀ-MĀLAI."

The *Pura-porul Venbā-Mālai* is a very ancient work, professing to be founded upon a still older composition called "The Twelve Chapters," by one of the twelve disciples of *Agastiyar*.* This points to a mythic origin, but we cannot historically go further than its Tamil author, or compiler, as he would represent himself. It is quite essential for a Tamil writer who would become a classic to cite his original, or the authoritative first work from which he draws (or professes to draw) his materials. (See *Nannûl*, 4-10, and Pope's *3rd Grammar*, p. 142.) Where there is no such first work (முதனூல், Mutanûl), he or his commentators must suppose or invent one, and ascribe it to some venerable personage. The real author here is AIYANĀRITHAN, of whom nothing is known but that he is said to have been a descendant of the old C'era kings, and the compiler of this very interesting composition. It can hardly be less than ten centuries old. / It has recently been for the first time printed under the editorship of Ve. Svāmināthaiyar of Uttamatâna-puram, the very learned and worthy Tamil Head-Pandit of the Kumbakonam College;† and has probably never been seen by any European till now, though the late Sir Walter Elliot (*clarum et venerabile nomen*) obtained and caused to be translated some fragments of it. These were edited for private circulation by R. Sewell, Esq., M.C.S. Some were also printed in the Asiatic Quarterly.

Mâlai means 'garland.' *Venbā* (see Pope's *Kural*, Int. xxv and *Nāladi*, Int. xxvi) is the name of the metre—very artistic quatrains like those in the *Nāladiyār*.

---

* In the commentary on the *Tol-Kāppiyam* by Nacchinârkkiniyar, Porul-athi; ix, 94 (C. V. Tāmotharam Pillai's edition, p. 807, Madras 1885, reference is made to this statement.

† Now of the Madras Presidency College.

Poruḷ is a subdivision both of grammar and of treatises in general, and signifies 'substance, reality, subject.' This *Poruḷ* is divided in the most ancient grammar, the *Tolkāppiyam*, into Agam ('inner') and Puṟam ('outer'). Of these, *Agam* ('the *subjective*,' treats of love, its various emotions, incidents and accidents. *Puṟam* ('the *objective*') relates to all 'other things'—life in general, and especially war, and the affairs of kingdoms. This work, though professing to treat of practical subjects in general (*Puṟam*), has portions, as will be seen, which belong to the other division (*Agam*)—emotional and passionate. The ideas and even the phraseology of these verses are cited and used by all commentators upon the other classics, as being of absolute authority.

It is divided into twelve chapters (Paḍalam: Skr. पटलं), or as they are generally termed, *Tiṇai* (திணை)*, containing 360 quatrains.

It seems probably that the work itself is more ancient than the Kuṟaḷ, and suggested many of its couplets. It is closely allied in subject and in tone to the *Puṟanāṉūṟu*. (P. N. N.), with which and the Tol-kāppiyam it must be studied, though it is more recent than the *text* of these works.

It will be necessary to give some account of the Puṟa-Nāṉūṟu, or "Four Hundred Lyrics of Life.' This anthology has been lately printed for the first time, though it has been in existence for upwards of a thousand years, and contains ballads which in substance must have been sung in the early centuries of our era. We owe it also to Svāminātḥaiyar, the learned and indefatigable Professor of Tamiḻ in the

---

* *Tiṇai.* This much used Tamiḻ word-of-all-work really signifies 'genus,' and is applied to the main divisions of any subject. These are divided into sections (*tuṟai* = துறை). This latter is equal to 'species,' and is used for the subdivisions of a subject. Here, each chapter is preceded by a small summary; and every quatrain has a curious little couplet giving the pith of the quatrain. This couplet is called *Koḷu* (= substance, contents: from கொள்).

Kumbakonam Government College, that it is now carefully edited and put forth with all necessary apparatus in such a way that it may find an entrance into the house of every Tamiḻ scholar. This is the fifth large work issued by the same editor. The industry and learning which have been employed in the editing of these books would have gained for Svāmināthaiyar a very high place among scholars in Europe, if the subject had been one which the scholars of the West were disposed to value. But, although the very ancient, copious, and refined Tamiḻ language is inferior to none, it is regarded by most people as the (probably barbarous) vernacular of a people living somewhere in a remote district of Great Britain's imperial possessions. Neither does our Indian Government nor do our Universities fully recognise the value of Tamiḻ literature; and so those who spend their lives in the study of the great South Indian classics must resemble men seeking for pearls under water. Our editor's compatriots, however, will not be slow to recognize the benefit that his studies are conferring upon his people. Nor is it too much to hope that his labours may be so far recognized as to procure for him such pecuniary assistance as may save him from absolute loss. Tamiḻ scholarship is a direct road to poverty!

To return from this digression. This work consists of 400 Lyrics, varying in length from six lines to fifty, being for the most part songs sung by Court minstrels and wandering bards in honour of the kings of the South, including not only the Pāṇḍiyan, the Cōḻan, and the C'eran kings, but about 120 of the petty Rājās and chieftains who then divided the South, and were more or less independent, having their fortresses on every hill and coign of vantage throughout the Southern land. Of these ancient rulers and heroes scarcely anything is known but what these, and a few similar works, enable us to conjecture. Their names have not yet been found or recognized in inscriptions or coins, and it is very doubtful whether we shall ever be able to recover many authentic details of their history. Still, the glimpses of ancient manners, thought, and conditions of life afforded by these poems are exceedingly in resting. The ancient bards about 150 in number, fragments of whose songs have thus been rescued, were of very unequal powers ; but some of them display, if I am not mistaken, very great poetical genius, and some of the fragments are veritable gems.

It is worthy of note, also, that of these poems, except the introductory invocation (which is of much later date, by Peruṉ Tevaṉār,* the translator of the Mahā-Bāratam), none make any decided allusion to Šiva worship. Demons are constantly referred to and various charms and ceremonies for driving them away from the battle-field, where it was their delight to hold their 'eery' festivals, are mentioned. Throughout all the petty kingdoms of the Tamiḷ lands, there seems to have been a system of demon-worship much like what now prevails in the extreme south.

Feasts and dances in honour of Murugan (from T. '*murugu*,' a fragrant wood: *Agullochum*) are often alluded to. He was evidently the tutelary god of the aborigines of the South, and is now promoted to be the younger son of Šiva.

I shall reserve a more minute account of these poems, their heroes and their bards, for another occasion, and return at once to the *Puṟa-Poruḷ Veṇbā-Mālai.*

[* He seems to have edited a series of works for the Madura literati.]

PAḌALAM I.

Veṭchi, OR THE CATTLE-RAIDERS.

The first *tiṇai* is called *Veṭchi*, and the following seven divisions have titles of a similar import. They are taken from the garlands worn by warriors in the contests in which the tribes of South India in those times seem to have been incessantly engaged. The Tamiḻ rhetoricians enumerate eight species of distinctive garlands worn by kings and warriors when going forth on various expeditions, the garland being supposed to indicate the character of the undertakings, and the feelings of those engaged in them.

This is to us a novel form of the 'language of flowers.'

The *Veṭchi* (வெட்சி) is the *Ixora coccinia*, which is commonly called 'Flame of the Forest,' or sometimes 'the country geranium.' It bears a profusion of flowers, sometimes of quite dazzling brightness, and of a deep scarlet hue. These garlands were intended to strike terror into the eyes of the opposing hosts, and to some extent supplied the place of military uniform. The armies of Europe have never been unmindful of the moral effect of the soldier's head-dress; though it would be a novel experience if our troops went forth to war like a marching garden of flaming and fragrant flowers! The warriors who wore the *veṭchi* were cattle-raiders. It would seem that this constituted no small part of the duty —and duty was delight—of the ancient South Indian soldier.

This *Paḍalam*, or chapter, contains twenty-one verses, and illustrates with exceeding clearness several phases of the thoughts and habits of the people in those 'good old times'! A translation is given of the more important verses, and a summary of the remainder.

§ 1. *The King's Call to the Cattle-raid.*

VERSE 1. THE KING SUMMONING HIS PEOPLE.

"Youthful warrior, who bearest the wondrous three-pronged dart, go forth, seize and bring home the herds of cattle with the bulls their leaders! See your foes bending their bows, as though they would cut down whole forests and set them on fire, and inspecting their arrows as they fit them to the string. Put their ranks to flight!"

§ 2. *The Toddy-booth.*

This introduces the idea, which is always coming to the front in these poems, of the 'toddy-jar.' [§ 15.] The raid begins and ends with the *canteen*.

VERSE 2.

"Forget not, O thou with the loving large eyes, the clear sweet boiled palm-juice in the standing jar of toddy, never empty. The warrior on whose feet are the heroes' anklets, who is fierce of eye, endures not debt. To-morrow's morn shall see the foeman's herds thronging thy wide-extended gates."

It would seem that these champions cleared off their scores with the nymph of the palm-wine jar by means of the plunder they brought home. [§ 16.]

All classes except Brahmans, even the ladies, are represented as indulging freely in the use of toddy. The same thing is illustrated in the Kambar-Rāmāyaṇam, where the whole Court—king, queens, princes, counsellors, and warriors—are represented as indulging in a most unedifying debauch of many days' duration. [Bāla-Khāṇḍam xviii: 'The Canto of the Festivities.']

§ 3. *Eager for the Fray.*

VERSE 3.

"The raven's hoarse cry arises in the jungles of our foes who own the beauteous herd—omen of ill to them; while beating their drums our warriors armed with long spears put on the *veṭchi* flower and go forth upon the well-nigh impervious paths, where the raven croaks." *

§ 4. *Omens.*

This speaks of *omens* which are continually referred to here.

* cf. P.N.N., 280.

Verse 4.

" In the little town encircled with barriers, at eventide, while our people stand around with clasped hands, she [the wise woman of the village] speaks, and would say, 'Bring forth toddy from the jar in the stand'; but really says, 'Bring the large-eyed cow from the shed.' Therefore, O thou who bear'st the bent bow in thy mighty hand the victory is ours." *

§ 5. *They go forth.*

The raiders armed with bows, and so styled in Tamiḷ, 'Ploughmen of the Bow' (cf. *Kuṟaḷ*, 872), go forth through the stony wilderness to the hill fortress of those whose cattle they are bent on carrying off.

Verse 5.

"Like death's satellites, bearing the curved bow in their left hands,
followed by flocks of vultures they go forward!
Their minds fixed on the station where the herds of cattle are found,
they make for the hill whereon the long *bambus* wave."

§ 6. *The Scouts.*

The raiders send forward trusty spies to ascertain the precise position of the bell-bearing herds, and the number of the warriors to whom these belong.

Verse 6.

" Our friends have gone forth in the deep darkness to ascertain,
the place of the herds, and their number, and the hosts
of the bowmen who defend them, O eagle-eyed warrior king,
with honey-dripping wreath, and hero's jewelled anklet deckt ! "

The raiders lie hidden in the dense jungle at the foot of the hill, while the scouts make their way through the darkness up the gorge, to spy out the dwelling-places of those against whom the foray is made.

***Here தொழு = 'stand', or 'cowshed'; குடக்கள் = 'toddy from the jar,' or " large-eyed "; and for ஈ they heard ஆ = 'cow': so she seemed to say, 'Bring the large-eyed cow from the fold.' The sybil seemed involuntarily, by the mistake of a letter (ā for ī), to urge them to the raid.**

§ 7. *The Fort Surrounded.*

The raiders surround their enemies' fortified dwelling on the crest of the hill, and set guards to prevent egress on every side; and this is done in the silence of the night unknown to the unsuspecting objects of the attack.

VERSE 7.

"None from hence shall 'scape! Like fires of the day of doom
the enemy came forth at dawn. Their power is spent.
The stealthy marauders have surrounded every part:
none of the beleaguered ones shall issue forth."

After a short but fiery contest, the attacked have retired within their stronghold, which is straitly besieged.

§ 8. *The Storming of the Hill-fort.*

The raiders, urging on their swift-footed horses and bearing aloft their bent bows, storm the fort, which is soon enveloped in flames.

VERSE 8.

"Hate lends them help; while fierce fire rages they shout;
they rush on regarding no obstacle! In the broad daylight
those fall that living never knew defeat! With jewelled anklets' sound
and deadly bows the raiders storm the mountain fort."

§ 9. *The Seizure of the Cattle.*

Having overcome and taken the stronghold, the victorious heroes seize the whole herd—bulls and cows and calves.

VERSE 9.

"Like a congregation of spotted tigers, in the town
in midmost of the *bambu*-encircled upland plain
they take possession of the assembled herds, and round about
stand steadfast to repel all who would set them free."

§ 10 *The Fight around the Herds.*

Now muster on all sides the clansmen of the attacked, people wearing wreaths of *Karanthai* (கரந்தை, a species of *Basil*, bearing a dark purple flower). This wreath is worn by the bands that come forth to rescue the stolen cattle and repel the raiders. The whole subject is more fully treated in the second *Paḍalam.*

VERSE 10.

"Those, who came to retake the herds from the raiding host, have fallen ;
the vultures have swooped down upon the corpses of the slain ;
their dark clouds are like those of the arrows reeking with blood,
that the foeman, fearful as those of the cruel bowman death, have sent forth."

§ 11. *The Cattle driven off over the Wolds.*

The raiders, to elude pursuit, drive off the herd quietly through wild unfrequented paths.

VERSE 11.

"'Let the cattle graze, and rest awhile in quiet companionship' ;
thus spake the bow-bearing, jewel-ankleted hero, though he saw
the rescuing host rushing after, like water from a lofty hill ;
and so they paused under the shadow of the mighty crags."

§ 12. *The Raiders Return.*

The relatives of the raiders rejoice at the return of their hero with the spoils.

VERSE 12.

"First come the cows with their hanging dewlaps ;
then come the bulls with their black masses of hair.
The warlike drums sound out, and the wood-land maids
who feared for their loved ones hail the signs that show them safe."

§ 13. *The Spoil brought home.*

While the drums sound out, and the whole town is in a state of eager expectation, the raided herds enter the village enclosure.

VERSE 13.

"The hero's spouse, with shining rows of teeth and rare beauty,
sees her hero crowned with wreaths midst which the beetles hum !
Her heart swells with gladness as she beholds the herds
with tinkling bells filling the open spaces of the village."

This is sung of in P.N.N., 262 :—

"Bring out the buried *toddy*; slay the rams;
In *pandāl* thatched with green leaves, with slender *(bambu)* posts,
Lavishly strew fine sand from river-bed!
My lord, who first led the charge against the foeman's van,
Comes home in rear guarding the captured herds;
His faithful comrades march, more wearied than himself."

This is a song of Madura. Did even the Pāṇḍi kings indulge in these sports? See also P.N.N., 297.

§ 14. *Division of the Spoils.*

The raided herds of cattle are distributed among the successful soldiers according to each one's deserts.

Verse 14.

"To those who overcame with their glittering swords,—
to those who sought out as spies, and brought back the tale,—
to the skilful ones that interpreted the favouring omens,—
they divide the herds of cattle in the little town."

§ 15. *The Feast.*

The warriors with jewelled anklets, that tinkle as they walk, drink 'toddy,' and dance rejoicing.

Verse 15.

"The aspect of the maidens, sweet of speech and fair as *Lakshmi*,
fills with pleasing pains the warrior's soul!
The gladness of the intoxicating draught departs, as does the
anger against his foes from out his soul.
Love is lord of all."

§ 16. *Gifts.*

The spoils acquired in the raid are lavishly bestowed on all that ask.

Verse 16.

"The wealth brought back from the battlefield by the warriors
that flinched not in the strife, but bent their bows,
has become the price paid for the fiery drink
by musicians, drummers, singers and singing women."

§ 17. *Extra Rewards.*

To those who as scouts explored beforehand the scene of the fierce strife they give more honour than they take unto themselves.

VERSE 17.

"To those who feared not death, but night and day
explored the battlefield, spied out, and brought us news,
some gifts beyond those given to others surely is due,
O warrior wielding the keen dart, that slays the fiery foe!"

§ 18. *The Favourable Prognosticators.*

Some reward is given to those who faithfully expounded the lucky signs.

VERSE 18.

"When we went forth with minds intent upon our foemen's, herds,
these made plain the favouring signs, and sounds that gave us heart
think not of what is strictly due as their share; to each give
four cows, with udders large, distended with milk!"

§ 19. *The Drummer.*

The virtues of the old man who beats the drum, according to ancestral custom, for the jewel-ankleted warriors, are celebrated.

VERSE 19.

"For my grandsire's grandsire, his grandsire's grandsire
beats the drum! For my father, his father did the same;
so he for me. From duties of his clan he has not swerved:
Pour forth for him one other cup of palm-tree's purest sweetest wine!"

The following song (P.N.N., 290) illustrating the section is attributed to the ancient poetess Avvaiyār :—

"O king, whose chariot drawn by angry elephants
Is foremost in the fray, pour out for him the palm-wine.
His father's father, in fierce fight, when spears flew thick,
Died tenacious as the workman's pincers,
Defending the king, thy father's father!
He too with valour filled, instinct with glory of his race,

Shall, like palm-leaves that screen from sun's fierce rays,
Hide thy head from the spear hurled at it" *

§ 20. *The Demoness Koṟṟavai.*

Here they celebrate the never-failing grace of her who protects the warlike host, whose glory never grows dim.

VERSE 20.

"Her beauteous banner bears the lion's form. Her hand the golden parrot grasps and bounding stag.
A countless host of demons round her press—great Koṟṟavai!
When we designed the attack on the foeman's fort,
she went before our host, and made foes flee!"

§ 21. *The Devil-Dance.*

The damsels, with flawless jewels decked, dance the mystic dance with Velan, † now the deed is done. This is called the *Vallai Dance*.

VERSE 21.

"Did the black-throated One behold, he would rejoice;
it is the dance performed for the dart-hurling *Murugan*
by warrior, and by jewel-bearing lovely maid,
with fragrant garlands dight."

The following (P.N.N., 257) gives a potrait of the leader of the cattle-raid. It is somewhat confused, but belongs to the VEṬCHI Paḍalam:—

CALL THE MILK MAIDS!

"Softly he treads as though pebbles were in his sandals;
Huge his paunch and broad his chest,
Bright his eye, and beard bristly as the mountain-side,
His cheeks hang down like dewlaps!
Who is this that thus cometh with his bow? A fearful sight!
Look close, he doth not come from far:
He is not one whose fort is in the wilderness.
At early dawn he watched the course of the foeman's herds,
Pointed them out with his hand, numbered them,

* "He will cover thy head in the day of battle."

† *Velan* = spearman.

And with his bow drove off the would-be rescuers!
The herd is large, but what the gain
If those who milk with white large-mouthed vessels,
And who churn are not at hand."

These twenty-one verses form the whole *Paḍalam* commemorating the incidents of the cattle-raid.

PAḌALAM II.

THE *Karanthai* WREATH, OR THE RESCUERS.

This is a wreath of *basil* or *tulaci*, a sacred plant of several species having dark purple flowers, contrasting with the bright crimson of the *Veṭchi* of the former *Paḍalam*. This *Karanthai* wreath was worn by those who went forth to oppose the raiders and rescue the herds. In P.N.N., there are eleven lyrics referred to this *Tiṇai*.

§ 1. *The Karanthai.*

Here the owners of the herds with their chaplets of dark purple flowers rush forth to the rescue.

VERSE 22.

"The crowding warriors crown their heads with garlands of *karanthai*,
and go forth to rescue the herds the foeman drives away;
as though one should bring back the souls of dwellers on earth
begirt by the sounding sea, after death has devoured them."

§ 2. *The Summons.*

The people whose herds are being driven away are bidden to relinquish their occupations and haste to the rescue.

VERSE 23.

"The jewel-ankleted heroes, the fierce bowmen,
they who wield the spear, men terrible to sight, who fear not
death in their fierce anger,—all hear the sound of the drum,
and go to rescue the flocks which the veṭchi-chapletted have carried off."

§ 3. *The Rescuers on the Track.*

Only those unfit for war remain in the town; the rest, boiling with fierce wrath, follow the track of the raiders.

VERSE 24.

"The conch-shell sounds, with the mighty horn, and instruments of music;
adorned with peacock feathers, and roused by the roll of the loud drum.
The *Rescuers* arise, and over the fiery desert make their way,
following the tracks of the cattle,—spears glistening like the sun."

§ 4. *The Doubtful Fight.*

They draw near the raiders, surround them, attack them with fearful energy, and a battle with many changeful fortunes is fought.

VERSE 25.

"Like a multitude of tigers or lions or warrior-elephants,
full of power and wrath and honourable shame and glorious resolve,
they shout, and hasten on, as they hear
the raiders' defiant cry;—and so the battle rages."

The following sections of this chapter speak of the glory of the individual heroes on either side. They fall fighting to the last full of enthusiasm. But we shall henceforth content ourselves with a few specimen verses.

§ 13. *Glory of the King.*

The praise is sung of the *Maṛavan* king, a valiant swordsman.

VERSE 34.

* * * * * *

"They *truly live* who yield their lives fighting against the foe in the fierce battle amid the flash of swords and the whirling of the spear!"

§ 14. *The Heroic Race.*

The praises of the heroes of tried valour and of ancient race.

VERSE 35.

" The men of ancient race that appear foremost in the fight wielding their swords; who stand as, in the universal deluge, some mountain-top rises firm amid the flood;—
what wonder if their glory lives when all falsehoods have passed away!

Thus ends the chapter of the *Rescue*.

We have seen that many of the lyrics in the *Puṟa-nānūṟu* seem to have been composed from the hints given in these verses; or it may be that from those lyrics this more systematized work has arisen. Certain it is that they are closely connected, and must be studied together. Thus P.N.N., 259 evidently refers to an incident in the attempted rescue. The rescuers are in sight of the raided flocks, but the raiders themselves are not seen; the bard cries out to the angry pursuers :—

" See'st not the ambushed Maṟavars with well-strung bows,
Hid in the jungle vast amid the leafy trees,
Who while the raided cattle move, move not with them!
Stay, stay, all honour to thy glorious soul! O thou
Whose foot the hero's jewelled anklet wears, by whose side
Glistens the sword resplendent, whose steeds,
Quivering with eagerness, shake like the priestess' frame
Before the demon shrine, when *Murugan* inspires her soul!

Here we have an instructive glimpse of the current demon worship, with the agitated priestess dancing wildly before the image of the hill-god. This may be seen daily even yet in the South.

Cattle-lifting is the chief topic in all these poems. It was the beginning of warfare: the *Raid* was followed by the *Rescue*, and these by the organized *Invasion* of the enemy's country (for which another wreath was assumed). This leads to the systematic *defence*, and the defenders assumed a different wreath. The siege and protection of forts each demanded its appropriate garland. Then came *war in general* and for that another wreath was borne. And finally, the victors who had gained *supremacy* had another wreath, which they wore as the proud token of their victory. Thus our work relates to the expeditions in which these eight different chaplets were worn by the combatants. Some interesting chapters follow in which kings and their attributes, and miscellaneous matters connected with the life of the people, are illustrated. It is from these, as has been said, that the authors of the Kuṟaḷ, the Nālaḍiār, and other lesser poets drew much of their material. It must be evident, therefore, that in many respects the work we are now concerned with is an introduction to almost the whole of the genuine poetry of the Tamiḷ language.

The thorough exposition of these chapters, which reveal to us the South Indian primitive tribes making war with one another from their hill fortresses, would require a volume. It must be remembered that in those days there were three great kingdoms of the south—the Pāṇḍian, with Madura as its capital; the C'era, with Karūr as its centre; and the Choḷa dominion, with Uṟaiyūr as its chief town. (See my Nālaḍiār, p. 414; verses 240-3). But besides these, almost every little hill had its chieftain who sometimes considered himself subject to one or other of the great powers, but generally was independent, and sometimes even fought against them. These petty chieftains were for the most part of lower caste, if indeed caste distinctions was really recognized among them. In the greater kingdoms Brāhmanical influence was predomimant, and was gradually leavening the whole South.

The chief tribe of what we may call the aborigines were the Maṟavar, or 'men of violence,' as the name signifies. They often fought as mercenaries in the armies of the greater kings. They still form a very great part of the population of the extreme South, and have no small share of the rude qualities of their ancestors.

The Demoness whom they worship was called *Korravai*, (கொற்றவை) 'the Victorious One' [in Malayāḷam, Korri] (கொற்றி). She was evidently the object of worship among the oldest peoples of the South, and she is the great Demoness whose worship is performed under many names in the Devil temples which are still found in every southern village. The Brāhmans have transferred her attributes to Umā, the wife of *Šiva*, and call her *Durgā*, with whom she is now quite confounded.* There was also a divinity, the Hill-god of all the South, who is represented as being the son of *Korravai*. His name is *Murugan*,‡ 'the

---

* The whole history of the myths connected with *Durgā* and many kindred subjects should be studied in Muir's "Sanskrit Texts," vol. iv., with references to the very complete index.

‡ The following note was communicated by Mr. S. W. Coomāraswāmi to "The Light of Truth" Vol. III. p. 222.

The following information, which the Rev. Dr. G U. Pope of Oxford has kindly sent me in reply to an enquiry about the root-idea of முருகு, will, I hope, be of interest to some of the readers of your valuable journal.

"I think முருகு really means 'perfume,' and is thence given to the tree, under which dances in honour of their hill-deity were performed by ancient South Indians.

I am sorry to say that there is no great interest felt here in Tamil literature.

The glossaries to my Kural and Naladiyar have been carefully compiled.

On the strength of the above suggestion, the different meanings of the word in question may be, I believe, satisfactorily accounted for as follows.

முருகு (1) Perfume, or, by Synecdoche, a flower.

(2) 'Akil' (Agullochum), the wood being *sweet scented*.

(3) Honey, which is collected by bees from the *flowers* of plants.

(4) Toddy, which is sweet as *honey*, or which is obtained from the *spadix* of the palmyra or cocoanut tree.

(5) Youth or the *flower* of age. Compare also the expression the *bloom* or *bud* of youth.

(6) Beauty, which attends *Youth* and fades with age.

(7) Elevation (of mind) or high spirits, which distinguish youth from old age.

Fragrant One.' And he has been received into the Hindu Pantheon and invested with the attributes of *Kārttikēyan*, the warrior son of *Šiva*, and is so regarded by nearly all the rural tribes. Originally it seems quite certain that he had nothing to do with the Brāhminical deities. The student who would form an independent opinion on these subjects must read these verses in the original, comparing them with the *Puṟa-nānūṟu*, and with the *Tolkāppiyam* (*Poruḷ* 56—60), and with chapter I of the *Pattu-pāṭṭu* ('ten lyrics'). Good editions of all these have been issued by *Svāminātḥaiyar* and *Tāmotharam Piḷḷai*, veteran scholars, whose learning and industry are worthy of all praise. Of these works it is hoped that some account may hearafter be given. The dances in honour of these divinities, and

---

(8) Murugan or the Dravidian hill deity in honour of whom dances were performed under the *murugu* tree; or Karttikeya with whose attributes *Murugan* was invested after being admitted into the Hindu Pantheon. (Vide Dr. Pope's Extracts from Pura-Porul-Venba-Malai. Padalam 2nd Para, last but one.)

(9) A festival, originally dances and feasts in honour of *Murugan*; முருகியம் is a drum, probably used on these occasions.

(10) An ornament (for the ear), which adds *grace* or *beauty* to the person of the wearer.

முருகு—the lemon-tree has no connection with the above word but is an incorrect form of முருக்கு so called on account of the *thorns* common to that tree and the Indian coral tree or Moochie, which is very *fragile* and serves only for *fuel*. The root is முரு found in the verbs முருங்கு and முருக்கு respectively meaning to perish and to destroy.

In his edition of Nighandu 1st part, A. Kumaraswami Pulavar of Jaffna says that Murugan (Subramanya) was so called on account of his being the *younger* son of Siva.

As this explanation may not satisfactorily account for the application of the word Murugan to a demon or a demoniac, and as Murugan is represented as the son of Korravai or Korri, the great Demoness of the South, in Pura-Porul-Venba-Malai which is, according to Dr. Pope, more than a thousand years old, there can be little doubt that Murugan also was originally a demon of the South and that the name should be dealt with agreeably to this notion. [This is clearly erroneous. We will deal with the subject fully in the introduction.—J. M. N.]

especially of *Murugan*, are many, and are still performed. The late lamented *Sundaram Piḷḷai*, in an article published in the *Madras Christian College Magazine*, March 1891, has given an exceedingly interesting account of the *Pattu-pāṭṭu*, and he says: "It seems not altogether impossible that *Murugan* was originally a Dravidian deity; and that in the course of time, when Āryan civilization found it expedient to adopt the cult of the independent nations over which it came to exercise its influence, a place in the Purāṇic mythology was found for the war-god of the Tamils, as transformed and embellished by Āryan genius; just as in more recent times Buddhistic institutions and even Buddha himself, under the name of *Shashṭa*, came to be absorbed into Brāhmanism."

Perhaps one of the most remarkable 'developments' that can be found anywhere is that of the idea of this Devil-dance as seen to this day in the South, into the really beautiful idea of Šivan's mystic dance giving life and blessing to the whole created universe. This, most undoubtedly, is the origin of the dance in Tillai. [See *Nāl.*, 16.]

PAḌALAM III.

THE *Vañji* WREATH, OR INVASION OF THE ENEMY'S TERRITORIES.

Raids such as have been described naturally lead to systematic invasions of the territories of those who have proved themselves such troublesome and treacherous neighbours. The injured king now declares war, or makes war without declaring it: while he and his warriors, binding the *Vañji* wreaths upon their brows, go forth with their fourfold full array of elephants, chariots, horses, and infantry. The *Vañji** is the general name for any creeping plant, such as is

* Probably the Sanskrit 'Mādhavi' or *Hiptage madoblata*, a very large rampant shrub of scandent habit with lanceolate pointed leaves, seven inches long; handsome when in full blossom with its profuse trusses of white and yellow fragrant flowers, somewhat resembling the horse-chestnut, in the month of Feb.—J. M. N.

found on all the mountain slopes. This particular wreath is represented as composed of flowers of a yellow colour, and the plant is one whose leaves are green all the year round. It is the symbol of a race the fire of whose valour is never extinguished. It is curious that *Vañji* has become the poetical name of *Karûr*, the C'era capital, and it would seem that the C'era kings, of whom twelve are celebrated in the P.N.N., were remarkable for the frequency of their invasions of neighbouring territories. Being for the most part mountaineers, their energy was resistless, and we may add that their wrath was implacable. Thus in P.N.N., 4, the great poet *Paraṇar* sings of one of these expeditions, and his song is a specimen of very many in the same work. He celebrates the sword, the jewelled anklet, the capacious shield, the fiery charger, the resistless elephant, and the towering banner-crowned chariot of a king; and thus concludes:—

Like the ruddy sun arising over the dark sea
art thou in thy beauty, O king!
And therefore, the land of them that provoked thy wrath
shall ceaseless mourn, foodless, and helpless,
like the tender infant forsaken by its mother!"

§ 1. *The Invasion.*

The king puts on the unfading *Vañji* wreath, and contemplates the subjugation of the enemy's land.

[The invasion and complete subjugation of the whole southern seaboard by the famous Pāṇḍian *Nedum-çeḷiyan* is related in P. Pāṭṭu, vi, 149, etc.]

VERSE 36.

" Like young bulls red-eyed
the youthful warriors bend their bows,
with glistening eyes, longing for the battle-feast; and so
put on the *Vañji* wreath, to subdue the unsubdued."

§ 2. *The Invading Hosts.*

The heroes arise in their wrath, brandishing their bright swords, amid the trumpeting of the elephant-hosts.

VERSE 37.

"The drums sound out like the roaring of the angry sea!
Wreathed with the *Vañji* the valiant bands rush on.
In the midst of the glittering bands, like the eternal fires,
the elephants madly rush on like black clouds in the rainy sky."

The following verses speak of the uplifting of the banner, and the unsheathing of the sword. *Koṟṟavai* is again introduced as putting to flight the enemy's forces.

§ 6. *The Model Hero.*

VERSE 41.

"You ask how the hero distinguishes himself: he is
foremost, mid his kinsmen's hosts. He emulates the
prowess of the bravest. Like fire he penetrates the
foeman's rank: these are the deeds of the jewel-ankleted hero."

§ 8. *Woe to the Conquered.*

The soldiers commiserate the sufferings of the land they overrun.

VERSE 43.

"The lotus-like eyes of the warrior, whose breast bears
the warlike wreath, are wet with tears, as
he exclaims: 'They perish, a fearful spectacle to all beholders
they who erewhile rode forth with garlands gay,
with glistening eyes, and sound of warriors' cars.'"

§ 9. *The Rewards.*

As they come to distribute the spoil, the question arises, who of the foe shall be spared?

VERSE 44.

"Touch not the temples, where sacrifices are offered;
spare the dwellings of the holy ascetics;
enter not the houses of the sacred Vedic Brahmans.
Let all the rest be abandoned to our warriors as their guerdon.

[See P.N.N., 9.]

The vanquished enemy now submits and pays tribute. The prowess of the heroes is again celebrated.

§ 14. *The Wasted Land.*

The devastation of the ravaged land, and the deserted homes, described. [Cf. P.N.N., 6.]

Verse 50.

Spoils.

> "Gather the slaves, the heaped-up jewels, pearls,
> red gold, the plunder from the stately homes,
> and give them to the warriors ; while subjects
> of the hostile king make loud laments !"

The inhabitants of the invaded land flee on every side ; the country is ravaged with fire ; and the invaders build their fortresses.

§ 22. *The Warriors' Feast*

Verse 58.

> "The instruments of music sound out. The heroes like tigers rush
> upon the field and reap the crops and feast,
> while they explore the resources of the vanquished lands."

§ 23. *Glory to the Conquering Invaders.*

Triumph and pity mingle in the final song.

Verse 60.

> " Where palaces like mountains reared their heads, the roar
> of the consuming fire is heard. Wild jungle plants grow
> among the ruins. The conqueror rides glorious on his lofty car,
> round which triumphing hosts flow like a mighty sea !

These desolating wars account for the multitudes of deserted strongholds whose ruins are yet to be seen, and for the comparative sparseness of the population at the period when authentic history begins. In P. N. N., twelve lyrics refer to this chapter. In all the poems there is a note of an oft-times savage ferocity. These old Dravidians were great and most implacable warriors !

Whatever faults may be found with the government under the *Pax Britannica* by peevish and restless partisans, we see that the idea of a *Pax Tamuliensis* is a myth.

PAḌALAM IV.

The Kāñji Padalam, or the Defence of the Fort.

The Kāñji is the *Ulmus integrifolia*, or elm-tree, and its foliage was dark. Its flowers and leaves formed the wreaths worn by the defenders of an invaded country, and were supposed to be indicative of a stubborn resolve to conquer or die. This most generally ended in the death of the king and the overthrow of his kingdom, and hence the same word (Kāñji) is used for the wreath of a minstrel who inculcates moral precepts, and more especially dwells on the instability of wordly things. The word Kāñji has thus become a synonym for 'sober counsel,' and some of the verses under this heading have nothing particular to do with war. The great example of this is the Madura-Kāñji, an account of which will be given in the life of the Pāṇḍian, Talai-Ālaṅgā-nāṭṭu çeruvenṛa Nedum-çeḻiyan.

§ 1. *The Kāñji Wreath.*

The inhabitants of the invaded country put on wreaths of the *Kañji*, and retire to make a last stand in their mountain fortresses.

Verse 61.

"Since there is no longer any band to withstand the foe upon the plain,
at least we can die on the heights of our native hills!'
So saying, intent upon the defence of their little mountain homes,
the warriors assume the *Kāñji* wreath."

The following verses in the chapter illustrate the fierceness of the final struggle. Marvels of bravery are related. The heroes fall; their wives perish with them; the warrior rips open his wounds and dies on the plain; demons and demonesses brood over the gory battlefields, sometimes helping and sometimes destroying the dying men; much toddy is consumed, libations to the great demoness are poured out, and a universal wail is heard.

§ 19. *The Elegy.*

Praise and pity mingle in the song as the heroes ascend to the paradise of the valiant.

VERSE 80.

"He was the raft on which his people sailed over the sea of battle!
He was a pillar amongst the mighty!
He was the life of his town, and of the world!
The door of charitable deeds has been closed by the spear
that tore open our leader's breast!"

In P.N.N. there are forty-one lyrics, of which this gives the keynote.

Other topics are introduced, but the chapter ends with the 'crushing defeat' and it would seem, the extermination of the conquered people.

PAḌALAM V.

THE DEFENCE OF THE FORT.

THE *Nochchi* WREATH.

The next chapter speaks of the defence of hill-forts. When hostile kings besieged a fort, its defenders were accustomed to assume a wreath of the leaves and flowers of a wild tree called the *Nochchi*, or '*Vitex Nirgundi.*' There are many species of the *Vitex*, which is often called the five leaved chaste tree' (see Ainslie's "Materia Medica," vol. ii, p 252). The flowers are of a pure, pale-bluish colour, and have a pleasant fragrance. This flower is very celebrated in Tamiḷ songs. The poet Moçi-çāttanār has sung of it very sweetly (P.N.N., 271, 272):

"Like linked gems are *Nochchi's* curling ringlets blue,
Mid all the flowering trees is none whose tender hue
So fills the soul with love as thine, whose blooming wreath
Men see the youthful maiden's slender form ensheathe,

In the wide guarded city,—sight beloved of all;
And when fierce enemies attack the moated wall,
The warriors on their brows thy flowers defiant show,
As sign they shield their virgin fort from every foe."

It was the symbol of chastity, and those that wore these wreaths were pledged to keep their fort inviolate. The virgin fortress guarded by warriors so adorned, laughed at its foes. Much of romance mingled with the ferocity of those ancient days!

§ 1. *The* Nochchi.

The heroes go forth to guard their turret-crowned battlements, whence archers shoot forth their deadly arrows.

VERSE 86.

"Like the host of the *Avuṇar*, whose triple fort
the god with serpent crowned, and fiery form would take,
these warriors crowned with *Nochchi* wreaths
guard their strongholds, wielding the sharp-pointed dart."

This is one of the common places of Hindu verse, here borrowed from the *Mahā Bhārata*. The story of the destruction of the three forts of the *Asurar* (or *Avuṇar*) is most celebrated (see Muir's Sanskrit Texts vol. iv, pp. 203, 225).

There were in the sky three cities of the valorous Asuras, one of iron, another of silver, and a third of gold which Maghavān (Indra) could not demolish, with all his weapons. Then all the great gods, distressed, went to the great Rudra (afterwards known as Ṣiva) as their refuge and said to him after they were assembled: "Rudra, there shall be victims devoted to thee in all the sacrifices. Bestower of honour, destroy the Daityas with their cities and deliver the worlds." He, being thus addressed, said, "So be it"; and making Vishṇu his arrow, Agni, its barb, Yama, the son of Vivasvat, its feather, all the Vedas his bow, and the excellent Sāvitri (the Gāyatri) his bowstring, and having appointed Brahmā his charioteer, he in due time pierced through these cities, with a three-jointed three-barbed arrow, of the colour of the sun, and in fierceness like the fire which burns up the world. These Asuras with their cities were there burnt up by Rudra. [Cf. Tiruvāçagam, xiv.]*

One of the most famous historic defences of a fort is referred to in P.N.N., 21. The fort was called Kāna-pêreyil, and its king bore the epithet of *Véngai-mārban* (he whose breast wore a *Kino* garland). It was besieged by the famous king of Madura, *Ukkira-peru-Vaḻuthi*, of whom something will be said in the Analysis of the P.N.N. The poet ***Mūlam-kiḻar*** of ***Aiyār*** enumerates the parts of the fortification: "There was first of all, a moat so deep that it reached down to the abodes of demons; next there was a wall that rose up to the heavens; this was crowned with turrets from which the archers shot forth their arrows; there was an impervious wood that surrounded all; and there were numerous small forts at every angle."

The chapter contains the usual praises of the king and his warriors, relates how they fell fighting to the last: "they desired not, these lions in the fight, to guard their bodies or their lives." There is also a hint that these sieges were often the result of a refusal on the part of the king to give his daughter in marriage to the leader of the besieging army.

PAḌALAM VI.

THE BESIEGERS: ATTACKING ENEMIES' STRONGHOLDS.

THE *Uḻiñai* WREATH. [Veṇbā, 95-126.]

When an army marched to besiege a fort they wore a wreath of the Uḻiñai (*Oerua lanatar*), a species of cotton-

* Now printing at the Oxford University Press. [For the inner meaning of this allegory, and the Vedic passages referring to them, vide Siddhānta Dipikā Vol. II. pp. 90 and 91 and my Thesis read at the Calcutta Convention of Religions, Vol. X. No. 1.—J. M. N.]

plant, which is mentioned in P. N. N., 50, where it is said to have 'golden shoots,' and to belong to the 'Western Country.' This seems to have been worn by our heroes in derision, implying the worthlessness and weakness of the fort they went to seize. There is little remarkable in this chapter. We are told in it that sheep were offered in sacrifice by the combatants; the exploits of Vishṇu, who stormed a fort called *Viraço*, are celebrated; as also those of Śivan (as above). The encircling wood is cut down; the besiegers make rafts on which they pass the moat; scaling ladders are applied to the wall; the besiegers leap down into the area; tremendous fights take place; and the fort is taken.

§ 23. *Utterly waste.*

This relates how the conquerors, yoking asses, plough up the foundations of the fort, and sow worthless jungle plants upon the spot.

Verse 120.

> "The beautiful homes with pictured walls are levelled with the dust;
> asses are yoked to plough up the soil with spears;
> while worthless plants are sown on the foundations.
> Thus rages the conquering king!"

Other verses tell how there is a solemn washing of their blood-stained swords in sacred waters, and their presentation as offerings. The conqueror is solemnly wedded to the newly-acquired country; neighbouring kings bring tribute; and the chapter ends with universal submission: "They make a desert and they call it peace."

This subject is formally discussed in *Tolkāppiyam*, Poruḷ, 66-68, pp. 135-146. An admirable illustration of it is found in P. Paṭṭu, vi, 149, etc.

PAḌALAM VII.

WAR IN GENERAL.

THE *Tumbai* WREATH.

When a king contemplated an offensive war he assumed a wreath of the especial war-flower, the *tumbai (Phlomis Indica).** This is celebrated in Sanskrit as the *droṇa.*

§ 1. *The Wreath.*

VERSE 127.

"The king, whose war-drum sounds like unceasing thunder from the stormy clouds,
contemplates war that shall bedew the battlefields with blood.
He has put on the warlike *tumbai* wreath, and leads forth his hosts eager for the glorious strife."

To these old kings the excitement of war was a necessity of life; it was only thus that the monotony of existence could be relieved. Yet the horrors of war are much dwelt upon in these verses, and the king is represented as hesitating and only deciding upon battle when its necessity was apparent. The twenty-five verses of the chapter present, without any attempt at arrangement, many of the striking incidents of ancient war.

§ 2. *Presents to the Troops.*

The king heaps upon his chosen warriors gifts so that they go forth joyously under his banner.

VERSE 128.

"Badges of victory, lands, precious treasure, farms,
murderous elephants, and horses,—the king distributes.
His enemies, tho' strong in horses and chariots, tremble when
they hear of the movements of the jewel-bearing king."

§ 3. *Can the fight not be prevented?*

Both armies are brave: might it not be well to avoid a struggle?

---

* More correctly, Leucas Linifolia, Spreng.

VERSE 129.

"Should these warriors meet on the demon-haunted battle-ground
and with their polished spears begin the fight,
't will prove the saying false, that 'glory of the king
is guardianship of human lives.'"

Praises are now sung of the elephants, the horses, the gallant heroes, and the war chariots.

§ 9. *The Bard's Eulogy.*

The battle has been fought, and the bards on the battle-field burn or bury the dead with appropriate songs of praise.

VERSE 137.

"The tender spouse, the mother, the children know not this!
Upon the battle plain the fiery piles are lit, the death songs sung!
Heroes who fell beneath the elephants they slew
have gone to banquet with the heroes' gods!"

While demon shapes like fantastic shadows dance before, behind, and around, the bodies of some of the slain heroes are carried home.

§ 23. *Joy mingled with wailing.*

The wife, seeing the body of her husband covered with glorious wounds, and still grasping the sword, weeps with proud joy.

VERSE 151.

"Even death is abashed, for here is valour greater than his own!
The wife takes the sword from the hand of her dead warrior;
and, watching his calm triumphant repose, is glad as she bedews
his breast with tears."

This ends up with her voluntary death.

§ 25. *All died gloriously.*

They perish not; their renown is established for ever, though they lie strewn over the battle-field.

VERSE 154.

"They urged a stubborn fight alone, the two kings fell,
grasping still their spears; the earth is desolate!
Swiftly their wives uprose, and threw themselves into the flames.
Behold, even fierce death himself is satisfied."

This last verse seems to be a reminiscence of the history referred to in P.N.N., 62, 63. There the kings were the C'eran prince Kudakko-Nedum-C'eralāthan, and his rival the C'olan Peruviral Killi, who fell on the same battle-field. Their deaths were sung by the poets *Kalattalayār* and *Paranar*.

There is power and pathos in the following dirge, by the former of these:—

P. N. N. 62.

"What has become of the defiant valour of these rival kings?
Demon Furies probe deep the wounds of the fallen heroes.
While with bloody hands they besmear their dishevelled locks,
hovering round they display their blood-stained forms.
With sullen sound the death-drums moan, while demons dance.
The kings themselves raging with heroic wrath are fallen and lie amid the vultures that devour the slain.
The victory vaunting kingly canopies are low, the drums
that erewhile announced the leaders' glory and their sway, lie broken there.
Over the field, where myriads fought, a fearsome stillness broods.
The heroes' wives on dainties feast no more, nor bathe in perfumed waters, but lie dead on the bosoms of their lords.
They have gone to feast in the world of the gods,
who wear unfading wreaths from the tree of Immortality,—
whose eyes slumber not,—who eat ambrosial food.
Let the glory of the heroes live for aye!"

The site of this famous battle is unknown, but it is often referred to in old Tamil verse.

PADALAM VIII.

THE CONQUEROR.

THE *Vāgai* WREATH.

The leaves and flowers of the *vāgai* (*Mimosa flectuosa*) which are white, were worn by victorious kings, or any who won prizes in a competition. This chapter contains thirty-four verses, and appears at first sight to be entirely without plan or purpose; but it indicates the course of conduct which entitles any one, of any caste or class, to the praise of his fellow-men. It is probably of later introduction. There are more conquests than men are apt to imagine. Peace has its victories, more worthy of the Vāgai than those of war. A few of these verses, more artificial than the preceding, throw light upon the feelings and habits of the people, and these I have given.

Much of this is from Manu (or similar works), and is the introduction of the Brāhman code into the South. We have here the four castes, Kshatriyas, Brāhmans, Vaisyas, and Sūdras.

§ 2. *The King's Vāgai. Tirumphant Wār. The Kshattriya.*

The king, returning from conquest puts on the white ***vāgai*** garland, with the dark jewelled anklets, and girds himself with a purple cincture.

VERSE 156.

"These were the glorious wounds I received on the battle-field;
of them and sorrows we will think no more!
Bid my heroes who have overcome the fiery foe put on
the victor's anklets, stainless wreath, and girdle's purple folds."

Eight more verses similar to those in the foregoing chapters celebrate the kingly warrior's triumph.

The Brahman's Vāgai: Sacred Rites.

The learned Brāhmans celebrate their victory by offering the ***yāgam*** sacrifices.

VERSE 163.

"On the land bordered by the sea, on whose borders the surges rise,
he who has seen the Vetham's farthest shore, sits an *ascetic king*.
He, mid the praises of all, lights his sacrifieial fires, himself the shining light of men."

§ 10. *The Merchant's Vāgai: Practical Life.*

This speaks of the sixfold deeds of the merchant-king free from all evil.

VERSE 164.

"He ploughs and reaps the harvest; guards the lowing kine;
sells piles of precious wares; learns lessons of sacred lore;
performs his daily rites with the three fires;
scatters his gifts, nor looks for recompense:
he is the *merchant-king*."

These are the *Vaisyas*. They are the capitalists, proprietors; and the *Veḷḷāḷars* are their servants.*

§ 11. *The Veḷḷāḷar Vāgai: Faithful Toil.*

The Sūdras, or fourth caste, are those who cultivate the soil under the direction of the higher castes. Their 'triumph' (*Vāgai*) is to do the will of their lords.

VERSE 165.

"They flourish, in obedience to the three higher ranks;
according to the orders of these they act, and refuse no command;
they live according to the ethic rules prescribed;
they plough the fields, where the beetless hum;
they are the *life* of all that live on the earth."

§ 12. *The Chieftain's Vāgai: Conciliation.*

Here is a warning to the chief. He must never be tempted, contemplating his own fame and greatness to treat others contemptuously; but must learn to honour all men.

VERSE 166.

"Glorying in thy hosts, like the billows of the sea,
despise not thy foes! Those who rightly judge
touch not with their hands the fire that smoulders still,
'neath ashes white; but wait till it utterly dies out."

---

*[Dr. Pope is certainly wrong here. As will be seen from the passage in the Paṭṭinapālai quoted in Tamilian Antiquary No. 2, p. 17, Veḷḷāḷars are assigned all the three duties stated in this verse and they could not therefore be the servants of the Vaisyas; more of this in the Introduction.—J. M. N.]

The power of vanquished enemies may yet revive; even in their ashes "live their wonted fires."

§ 13. *The Wise Man's Vāgai: Truth.*

VERSE 167.

"The sun sheds light and scatters darkness in three worlds, earth, hell, and heaven.
The wise man knows three times,—the past, present and future belong to man.
Though sun, and worlds, and times should change and pass, though milk become sour,
and light darkness,—*the good man's word of truth fails not.*"

§ 22. *The Glory of the Heroic race: its Vāgai.**

The hero's mother speaks:

VERSE 176.

"My *father* lives in stone, a hero's effigy; my *husband* fell in battle slain.
My *brothers* died, resisting the foe to the last. When all the host had perished,
My *son*, like a porcupine, pierced by innumerable darts, fell fighting against the foeman's king."

---

* The previous stanza displaying the heroism of the ancient Tamil Dame should have also been translated. We give it below as also the corresponding verses from P.N.N.

21. *The Heroism of the Ancient Dame.*

The invading hosts she could not bear
Removed she the son from her suckling breast,
Handed him the victorious spear straightening it
Pointed to the stones of his ancestors
This ancient dame bade him go to the fight.

P. N. N. 278.

Her veins protruded, her flesh hung loose,
This ancient dame, she heard her son had turned
And fled from the battle-field; she was angered;
If this be so, she vowed she would cut off the breasts that suckled him;
With a sword in hand, she searched the bloody field,

§ 23. *The Town of the Heroes: its Vāgai.*

VERSE 177.

"Once in *village* courtyard children fitted their arrows to their bows,
to shoot the hares that gathered there. Its heroes now ward off
the strokes of hostile kings, from the mighty breasts
of their own leaders: such is the *city* now!"

§ 30. *Excellence is Victory. The Vāgai of the Good.*

VERSE 185.

"They change not as in the sky the changing moon.
Though they obtain wealth brought in ships from over the ocean,
Will their excellence change, whose hearts are pure
As the white conch-shell found on that ocean's shore?"

§ 33. *Grace in Life and Death. The final Vāgai.**

This chapter, concerned with the conqueror's wreath contains many verses that hardly seem to belong to the subject, and seem to be of later origin; but it ends with the

Among the slain she found her son severed in two
Then her joy was greater indeed than when she bore him.

P. N. N. 279.

Our heart ceases at this dame's great courage.
Well may she merit her ancient age.
In a former war, her father it was
Who, killed by an elephant, died in the field.
It was in the other day's battie, her husband
Fell overpowered by numerous hosts:
And now to-day at the beat of drum,
Delighted and yet how sad was she this woman with an only son.
She lovingly oiled and combed his hair,
Gave him his spear and bade him seek the battle-field!

* In the midst of life, we are in death. This is the keynote of the Hindu's character. His religion absorbs him in every station of life. As set forth in the next Paḍalam, the kings renounced their station after sometime. The previous verse is as follows:

" Old age comes on; the youth is past.
Disease comes on a pace. It is time
The five senses do not overpower us.
To search the twenty-five tatvas is wisdom."

following quatrain, which is meant to teach *there is no real victory but that which overcomes the world.* There is an aroma of the Bhagavat Gītā here.

VERSE 188.

"Before the body perishes, that long has afflicted us
with many pains and bound us fast, let us escape from the net,
with many meshes, of the world, which is full of fear and confusion,
and gain the right path! *This alone is strength and victory.*"

This ends the eighth chapter; the eight wreaths of the warrior have been sung in order.

PAḌALAM IX.

ROYALTY.

This chapter, in fifty-one quatrains, is supposed to treat of the duties and glories of the king and kingdom. The *Kuṛaḷ*, ch. xxxix contains the substance. It is entirely miscellaneous, and its topics will better be studied in connection with the Puṛa-nānūṛu (cf. P. N. N. 6).

A few verses illustrating the lives of these old chieftains are interesting. In P. N. N., 239, is given a picture of what to them was a 'perfect life.'

THE PARAGON.

"He wedded one with armlets decked, one fair to see;
He put on chaplets in the pleasant flowery park;
He smeared himself with fragrant *sandal* paste;
He slew his foes with all their kindred race;
He friends extolled and magnified;
Homage to none he paid as mightier than himself;
Triumphed o'er none as weaker than himself.
He ne'er sought aid of others as a suppliant;
To none that asked did he refuse his aid.
He shone with glory in the councils of the state;

He stood a bulwark, 'gainst the vanguard of the foe;
He followed up relentlessly their fleeing host.
He urged his charger swiftly o'er the plain;
Round the long course he drove the lofty car;
He rode aloft on mighty elephant of state;
He quaffed from golden bowl the sweet palm-wine;
He made the hearts of minstrels glad with feasts;
His lucid word made clear the darkest theme:
And thus, all that a man may do he did!
Take ye the head of this all-glorious one,
Cut off with sword, or burn, or let it lie
Where'er you will; his glory is *secure*."

The king was *Nambi Neḍum Ceḻiyan*, evidently a king of Madura in very ancient days. He is mentioned nowhere else. The minstrel was *Muṟuvalār* ('the laughing one') of *Pêreyil* (see notes on v. 36), and this is his only remaining song.

The following beautiful verse (P. N. N., 245) is by *Mā-Kothai*, the *C'eran* king, on the death of his queen:—

" My sorrow swelling knows no bounds, but hath not strength to free me from this loathed life! I bore her forth to burning ground, where Kaḷḷi* spreads; there on the fire
I saw the fuel heaped; I laid her on her couch
Of rising flame! The innocent in soul hath died,
And left me here! What charm hath life henceforth for me?

These kings not unfrequently renounced their kingdoms and became ascetics. This is referred to in the two following songs. (P. N. N., 251, 252.)

THE KING HAS RENOUNCED HIS KINGDOM AND BECOME AN ASCETIC.

" We saw erewhile the king within his pictured home
weaving gay garlands for the happy mountain maids;
but now, upon the mountains in the *bambu* brake
amid the waterfalls, he dwells; and lights his fire
with wood† the elephants have brought
and dries his tangled hair."

---

* A kind of Euphorbium, abundant in desolate places.

† Wild elephants serve the holy ascetic.

"Amid the roaring cataracts he makes his way;
his hue is changed; his locks are brown as *Tillai* buds.
He plucks the creepers' sacred flowers.* But erst he wove
the net of courtly words that took the simple hearts
of the fair maidens in his stately palace-home."

The following lyric (P.N.N., 243), which strikes a chord that will vibrate in many hearts, was *Toḍi-talai Viḻu-Tanḍinār*, one of the bards of the ancient Madura College.

"I muse of YOUTH! the tender sadness still
returns! In sport I moulded shapes of river sand,
plucked flowers to wreathe around the mimic forms:
in the cool tank I bathed, hand linked in hand,
with little maidens, dancing as they danced!
A band of innocents, we knew no guile.
I plunged beneath th' o'erspreading myrtle's shade,
where trees that wafted fragrance lined the shore;
then climbed the branch that overhung the stream
while those upon the bank stood wondering;
I threw the waters round, and headlong plunged
dived deep beneath the stream, and rose,
my hands filled with the sand that lay beneath!
Such was my youth unlesson'd. 'Tis too sad!
Those days of youth, ah! whither have they fled?
I now with trembling hands, grasping my staff,
panting for breath, gasp few and feeble words.
And I am worn and OLD!"

[Cf. Nālaḍiyār, ch. ii.]

The young prince to whom this was sung was *Perum C'attanār* of *Olli-ûr*, whose dirge (P.N.N., 242,) was sung by Nallāthanār. It is as follows:—

"The youths wear garlands bright no more;
the damsels gather flowers no more;
the bard puts wreaths around his lyre no more;
the songstress gay adorns herself no more!
Cattle is dead, who with his mighty spear
O'ercame and slew great heroes, triumphed so!
O jasmine, dost thou flourish still in land of Olli-ûr?"

* The *Tāḷi*, a convolvulus, sacred to Šiva. (See Tiruvāçagam xix. 36).

PAḌALAM X, XI, XII.

MISCELLANEOUS.

These three chapters form a kind of appendix, into which much has been thrown that belongs properly to the other great division of *Aga-poruḷ*. There are however, a few verses that throw light upon the ancient history of the South. We have seen the warriors crowned with eight different wreaths. There are three flowers worn only by kings.

§ 1. *The Palmyra Wreath of the C'eran.*

The C'era king, when he went forth to war, assumed wreath of the flowers of the palmyra-tree,* which, flourished most in the lands over which he then held sway.

VERSE 240.

"By the gushing waters of the hill of Kolli,†
where the Kānthal‡ spreads its leaves like a canopy,
the Vānavan ‖ crowns his brows with the cool blue-lotus;
when he goes forth to war, his wreath is the palmyra-flower."

§ 2. *The Margosa Wreath of the Pāṇḍiyan : Vêmbu.*

The Pāṇḍiyan wears the Margosa§ wreath when he goes forth to battle.

VERSE 241.

"The great Vaḷuthi, ¶ the guardian just, the horseman swift,
who leads forth a valiant host of stout warriors with Tumbai,
when he goes out to fight, with bannered chariot dreaded by his foes,
crowns himself with the Vêmbu wreath, praised by all."

---

* *Borassus glabelliformis.*

† A range of hills in the Salem district, belonging to the C'era kingdom.

‡ *Gloriosa superba.*

‖ The 'heavenly': an epithet of C'era kings.

§ The *Nim, Vembu*: *Melia Azadirachta* (Lin.). In Portuguese Amargozeria' and corrupted into Margosa. See my Nālaḍiyār Lex. (*in loc.*)

¶ An epithet of the Pāṇḍiyans 'shining'?

§ 3. *The Ātti* Wreath of the C'o̤lan.*

The *Ātti* is the wreath worn in war 'by the C'embiyan.'

VERSE 242.

> " The garland of the king of the land Kāveri's rushing flood, where heroes go forth on elephants, wielding the murderous sword, decked with the jewelled anklets, and brandishing their spears, is the *Ātti*."

In Dr. Hultzsch's " Epigraphia Indica," vol. ix, Nos. 22, 23, 52, are given three Tami̤l inscriptions found at Ki̤l-Muttugur (முத்தூற்றுக்கூற்றம்), in North Arcot, of which one records the death of a hero who fell while rescuing some cattle that had been lifted (தொழுக்கொள்ள மீட்டுப்பட்டான்). The stone bears the effigy of the hero in relief. Some of these fallen warriors have offerings by their side. So in P. N. N., 232, ascribed to Avvai, it is said :—

> " Let change of morn and eve for ever cease,
> and all my days of earthly life be done ! For, ah !
> the stone stands there with feathers bright.
> Will he accept libations poured—he wont to give
> to all that asked—who now receives no gift bestowed ?"

There are many songs in P.N.N., bearing upon the same subject, and the photographs we possess of those recovered stones would be the most appropriate illustration of these verses.

In chapter X there are several verses which speak of the honour due to departed heroes. Surviving comrades seek far and wide for a suitable stone to place over the hero's ashes ; this stone is brought to the spot with great processions ; it is then washed and consecrated ; and finally inscribed with the hero's name and exploits.

---

* *Ātti* (*Bauhinia racemosa*), called also *Ār*. It is worn by Śiva.

§ 10. *The Setting up of the Stone.*

VERSE 251.

"While garlands wave, jewels tinkling sound and fragrant smoke goes up,
they pour forth libations of toddy, crown the stone with peacock-feathers, and inscribe it with their heroe's name, adding:
'This is the memorial of him who thirsted for the fight, full of valour, amid the hurling of the spears.'"

In some cases shrines were built, where the departed heroes were honoured. It would appear that while many widows died with their husbands, this was generally a kind of suicide, and not a formal *sati*. The *sati* was however, frequent, and in the P. N. N., Brahmans are spoken of as striving to hinder it, but in no case as prompting it. The life of the widow was depicted here as one of absolute asceticism, and to escape this many sought death.

We read (P. N. N. 246) of the Suttee (SATĪ), and this is hinted at in many of the verses.

The word Satī (सती)* is Sanskrit, and means a *virtuous woman*; but has been specialized to denote one who burns on the funeral pyre with her deceased husband. There is no word in Tamiḻ equivalent to it, nor is the custom at all consonant to the feelings of the Tamiḻ people. It was purely a Brahmanical idea. Yet there are evidences in the old Tamiḻ poetry that the widow felt herself a poor miserable outcast, and often sought relief in suicide. Many beautiful stanzas give utterance to this feeling. The tenderest affections of the human heart have often been perverted, and in this case the awful scenes of what in English we call the *suttee* had such an origin. Yet we must believe that in most cases the immolation was purely voluntary on the part of the victim

* The Skt. word *Sakti* (in Tamiḻ *Satti*) is the name of Šivan's 'energy' (see note 8 to life of Māṇikka Vāçagar), or bride Umai, who is also called *Sati*, and hence the words are often confounded.

—the result of over-exalted feeling. In the following verse the Brahmans and kindred of the despairing woman had attempted to dissuade her from the sacrifice; she replies to their urgent expostulations :—

P. N. N., 246.

"O ye of wisdom full! O ye of wisdom full!!
Ye bid us not go forth to death; ye would restrain,
O ye of wisdom full! but evil is your counsel here!
We're not of those content to live forlorn,
and feed on bitter herbs, here once they feasted royally.
We lie not on rough stones, who slept erewhile on sumptuous couch.
The pyre's black logs heaped up in burning ground
to you indeed seem terrible; to us,
since our mighty spouse is dead,
the waters of the pleasant lake where spreads
the lotus-flower, and the fierce fires are one?"

The queen supposed to utter these words was called *Perum Gôpendu* (=great queen), and her husband was the renowned *Bûtha-Pāṇḍiyan* of Madura.

In P. N. N., 255, the widow has found her husband's body amid the slain on the now lonely battlefield.

"If I should cry aloud for help I fear the tiger.
If I strive to bear him off, my strength fails me to lift his stalwart form.
May tremblings like my own afflict thee, pitiless death!
Were it not easy for thee to grasp my hand, and lead me to the shades?"

In P. N. N., 256, she appeals for burial with her lord :—

"O Potter, shaper of the Urn!
Like the little white lizard that sits
In the garland on the axle of the chariot,
Over many a desert plain I've come with him
Make the funeral urn large enough for me, too,
Maker of the urns for the old town's burning ground!"

6

In a quatrain (P. N. N., 234) the widow thus utters her lament :—

> "'T is sad! when we were young, the little white water-lily as wreath we wore ;
> But now our spouse, who lived in wealth and power,
> Is dead, and we drag on our painful days
> Eating the bitter grain from that same lily flower."*

In P. N. N., 249 is a picture of the surviving widow. The poor widow remembers the time—which seems but yesterday—when her royal spouse feasted many guests with rich dainties, and she enumerates especially the various kinds of rare fish taken from the royal ponds, for the banquet which she was wont to arrange ; but now,

> "The lady pure of heart, of radiant brow,
> Since HE has gone—entered the heavenly home—
> Sweeps a little spot free from ashes,
> And washes it with thickly falling tears!"

She is placing in the burial-ground the offerings of food (Piṇḍam) prescribed for the departed ones.

'The Sepulchral Urn' is the title of a chapter in Dr. Caldwell's "History of Tinnevelly," pp. 279-282. The subject of South Indian sepulchral urns is there discussed as far as the facts were then known. The learned author gives the Tamiḷ word for 'urn' as Tāḷi. It is so pronounced by rustics in Tinnevelly, but the real word is Tāḻi (தாழி). He thinks that these, as found in various parts of the country, are relics possibly of an antiquity higher than the Christian Era ; and he states that "No relic, trace, or tradition of such a mode of sepulture has survived to the present day." But in the Puṟa-nāṉūṟu (p. 228), and in other places, these urns are mentioned as used in the burial of heroes and kings at a period certainly not earlier than the eighth century A.D.

---

*The white water-lily yields a kind of bitter grain, which in times of mourning is eaten instead of rice.

A lyric addressed to the Chôḷa king, Kiḷḷi-Vaḷavan, by Muḍavanār of Aiyûr ("the lame bard of Aiyûr") is as follows:—

"O potter-chief![*] maker of vessels!
Through whose furnace sends up thick clouds
Of smoke veiling the outspread heavens,
Who makest vessels for the wide extended ancient town!
Thou art to be pitied! What toil hath befallen thee!
The descendant of Chôḷa kings,
Whose armies spread themselves to earth's utmost verge,—
Whom minstrels praise,—the truly glorious one,—
Whose glory shines afar,
As in the heavens the sun with resplendent ray,—
VALAVAN, the great, on the brows
Of whose warrior elephants bright banners wave,—
Hath gained the world of gods. And so
'T is thine to shape an urn, so vast
That it shall cover the remains of such an one.
But if thou would'st mould the needful urn.
The vast earth must be thy wheel,
And mighty Meru sufficeth not for earth to mould its form!"

The Bishop says that at the time when these urns were used, cremation must have been unknown, and burial the universal practice; but the two customs have ever existed side by side. The ancient inhabitants generally buried their dead, as will be seen by a careful study of Puṟaporuḷ Veṇbā; but Brāhminical and Ṣaivite usages were found side by side from very early times, throughout the South. It will be seen also by a reference to these two works (which are a mine of information regarding the ancient manners and customs of the southern lands), and from passages scattered through the other Tamiḷ classics, that when heroes fell in battle they were often buried on the spot, and their effigies in stone placed over the grave. The same was often done when kings and other great men retired into some lonely region (generally specified as the 'North,') and died there.

[*] It is curious that the title Kô = 'king, chief,' belong also to potters.

This is exemplified in the very touching histories of the king Kô-perum-Chôḷan and his devoted friends Pottiyār and Piciron. This illustrates Kuṟal, ch. lxxviii, 1.

> " Ye foes! stand not before my lord! for many a one
> Who did my lord withstand now stands in stone!"

Here the learned commentator, Parimelaḻagar remarks that when heroes died on the field of battle, it was the custom to place their effigies on the spot where they fell. These heroes often became tutelary divinities, or demons, and were worshipped with offerings of food and flowers.

In Puṟa-nānūṟu, song 218, the subject of worthy friendship is beautifully illustrated in connection with this topic. The renowned Kô-perum-chôḷan, who reigned in Uṟaiyūr, renounced his kingdom, went 'to the north' (the banks of the Ganges ?),* and died there. His most intimate friends, Pottiyār and Piciranthaiyār, who were not his subjects, shared his hermit cell, and all three after death were commemorated by stones placed side by side over their urns. The poet Kaṇṇaganār, visiting the spot, sang as follows :—

> " Red gold, and coral, pearls. and rare
> Gems the mighty mountains bare,—
> Remote their homes in sea or mine.
> If once the precious things combine
> And men in costly shapes entwine,
> Henceforth in blended beauty one they shine.
> So worthy men with worthy side by side
> Remain ; the worthless with the worthless bide."

The history of these three, as traced in P. N. N., is the favourite Tamiḻ illustration of faithful friendships (See Pope's *Kuṟaḷ*, ch. lxxix.) In Nālaḍi also, ch. xxi-xxiv, many exquisite thoughts on friendship are to be found.

---

* வடக்கிருத்தல் and not வடக்குப்போதல். It means residing on the north of one's place and starving oneself to death. This is done as a penance when one suffers a great reverse as in the case above. See a learned article on the subject in Sen Tamiḻ Vol. 8. No. 1. pp. 1 to 3.

THE 400 LYRICS:

"PUṞA-NĀNŪṞU".

PART II.

THE 400 LYRICS: PURA-NĀNŪRU.

This Agaval is by a minstrel, known to us as Kaṉyan or 'Singer' of the flowery hill, who was a court poet and friend of Kō-Perum C'ōḻan of Uṟaiyūr—a little, it may be, before the date of the Kuṟaḷ.

See Puṟa Nānūṟu, 67, 191, 192, 212.

ஞானிகள்.*

[192.]

யாதும் ஊரே;—யாவரும் கேளிர்;—
தீது, நன்றும் பிறர்தர வாரா;—
நோதலும் தணிதலும் அவற்றோ ரன்ன;—
சாதலும் புதுவதன்றே:—வாழ்தல்
இனிதென மகிழ்ந்தன்றும் இலமே;—முனிவின்
இன்னா தென்றலும் இலமே;—மின்னொடு
வானந் தண்டுளி தலைஇ யானாது
கல்பொரு திரங்கு மல்லல் பேர்யாற்று
நீர்வழிப் படூஉம் புணைபோல் ஆருயிர்
முறைவழிப் படூஉம் என்பது திறவோர்
காட்சியிற் றெளிந்தனம்;—ஆகலின் மாட்சியிற்
பெரியோரை வியத்தலும் இலமே;
சிறியோரை இகழ்தல் அதனினும் இலமே!

The Sages.

To us all towns are one, all men our kin.
  Life's good comes not from others' gift, nor ill,
Man's pains and pains' relief are from within.
  Death's no new thing; nor do our bosoms thrill
When joyous life seems like a luscious draught.
  When grieved, we patient suffer; for, we deem

---

*This was sent by Dr. Pope as a New Year's Greeting to all his friends in India in January 1906.

This much-praised life of ours a fragile raft
  Borne down the waters of some mountain stream
That o'er huge boulders roaring seeks the plain.
  Tho' storms with lightnings' flash from darken'd skies
Descend, the raft goes on as fates ordain.
  Thus have we seen in visions of the wise!—
We marvel not at greatness of the great;
  Still less despise we men of low estate.

Comp. Kural, 397, Paḷamoḷi, 116.

The Pāṇḍiyan Nedum Ceḻiyan.

In considering the kings and chieftains celebrated in ancient Tamiḻ song, the first place must be given to this great king and hero,—the Pāṇḍiyan Nedum Ceḻiyan, whose praises are sung also in the 'ten Tamiḻ Idylls.'* He is said to have gained a great victory in early life at a place called *Talai Alanganam*, where he defeated the C'era and C'oḻa kings, and seven other of the minor majesties of the south. He is lauded by four minstrels in this collection; but the late lamented Sundaram Piḷḷai Rai Bahadur, published articles in the 'Madras Christian College Magazine' (March and August 1891), in which, with an abstract of the lengthy poems in this king's honour (found in Pattu-Pāṭṭu), a summary of his history is given. Nothing could really illustrate the life and condition of ancient South India like a full and literal translation of all that has been sung in honour of this almost forgotten chief and warrior. It seems humiliating to record the fact that his name is found in no list of the Pāṇḍiyan rulers, and we are left to conjecture that it is but an epithet applied to him, while his real name has perished'. 'Ceḻiyan' means 'the Flourishing,' and is a title given to any of the Pāṇḍiyas, or Madura Kings; while 'Nedum' merely means 'tall' or 'great.' He is said to have been a

* This is the famous Pattu-Pāṭṭu, or ten songs. They are by different poets. In the paper on *Kabilar* an account of one of these is given: 'the highland song.'

great friend of poets, though nothing of his own has been preserved save one small but beautiful lyric. (72). His generosity was greatly celebrated.

The following lyric is addressed to this king by a poet, of whom nothing is known except the two poems in this collection. The verses in a remarkable way illustrate the supreme importance to the people of South India of Irrigation Works, which the poet is most anxious to impress upon the youthful sovereign, who was more given, it may be, to the shedding of blood, than to the construction of works for the distribution of water to the fields of his subjects.

The vast importance of irrigation has been recognised by all rulers of South India, though their constant wars have often prevented their doing efficiently what they knew should be done. This piece is in Tamiḻ a really magnificent bit of sage advice, expressed in highly poetical and forcible terms. The whole land was then as now divided into 'the good land' (*Nañjey*), or the alluvial soil along the banks of rivers and in the deltas, which could always be irrigated, provided the necessary reservoirs and anicuts were provided; and 'the poor land' (*Puñjey*), which was solely dependent on rain. Very extensive irrigation works were carried out by the ancient kings of South India, who had at their disposal large treasures and an immense amount of forced labour; but the works in the delta of the Godāvari and in the districts through which the Kāviri and its tributaries flow, are unrivalled in any age of South Indian history. Wherever this is attended to, the Government will be successful in securing the happiness of the people, who will not be ungrateful to those that secure their temporal welfare. An old Indian almost grudges any expenditure on the part of the Government which does not aid in bringing out the wonderful resources of the land. The great remedy against famine is, and always has been, irrigation. Considered in this light, this old lyric possesses singular interest.

On the Necessity of Irrigation.

[18.]

'Descendant of the Mighty Ones, who put beneath their feet
The wide extended earth, girt by the roaring sea.
Ten times a hundred million years
Prolonged be thy mighty sway!
Thou art the victor king of the city rich,
Whose moat is filled with both small and great,
Whose mighty guarded wall to heaven uplifts itself!
Dost Thou desire the wealth of all this world
And of the worlds beyond:
Or wish to overcome all Kings
And hold them 'neath Thy sway;
Or seek for glory and good renown?
Then Mighty Ruler, listen to my song,
Who give to frames of men the food
They need, these give them life;—
For food sustains man's mortal frame.
But food is earth with water blent:
So those who join the water to the earth
Build up the body, and supply its life.
Men in less happy lands sow seed, and watch to skies for rain,
But this can ne'er supply the wants of kingdom and of king.
Therefore, O C'eḻiyan, great in war, despise this not;
Increase the reservoirs for water made
Who bind the water, and supply to fields
Their measured flow, these bind
The earth to them. The fame of others passes swift away.

The C'ōḻan King, Kiḻḻi-Vaḷavan who fell at Kuḷa-muṟṟam.

This king is celebrated in eighteen songs, by ten different minstrels. One lyric (173) is ascribed to the king himself. *Kiḻḻi* was the family name of a renowned dynasty of *C'ōḻa kings,* eight of whom are mentioned in this collection. Its derivation is doubtful, but it may mean a digger, and is in fact a synonym of *Paḷḷava.*[1] He is said to have conquered the Cēra kingdom and taken Karūr, its then capital; and fell in battle at the village of *Kuḷa-muṟṟam* ('Pavilion by the Tank').[2] This portion of the anthology is of peculiar interest to Tamiḻ scholars.

The first song, relating to *Kiḷḷi-Vaḷavan* here is by *Ālattūr-Kiḻār* ('Lord of the Manor of Banyan-tree Town'), and is every way very noteworthy.

Ingratitude the only unpardonable Sin.

[34.]

' Whatever sins men do in hurting kine,—
All heinous crimes,[3] and wrongs to Brāhmans wrought,—
Where fault is pondered and confess't, a place
May yet be found to wash away the stain.
But they, who benefit conferred have slain
Can ne'er escape,'—so virtue's self hath sung.
O spouse of her with jewels rare adorned!
Each morn and eve at twilight hour, in song,—
With grain and flesh and milk and honey fed,—
I and my clan say, 'long live our king great Vaḷavan!'
In spacious court beneath the Itti's[4] shade,
The needful words of kindly courtesy,
He speaks with heart that knows no hidden guile,
And gives the minstrels feast of pure white rice,
Then lasting store of various wealth bestows!
If thus I sing not aye thy glorious might,
The lord of many rays shall know no rise.
Great king! I'm poor; but if the good

---

[1] The Tamiḻ root *paḷ* = *kiḷ*.

[2] Called also *Kurā-paḷḷi*. See 373.

[3] In the original: 'cutting the udder of kine, and procuring abortion.' Comp. Tiru-viḷai-āḍal, 26; Taylor's *Oriental Hist.* MSS. p. 75.

[4] The Itti or Iratti—a species of fig-tree.

In this world done by men of worth endures,[5]
Oh, may'st thou joyous live more years
Than are the rain drops, shed by sweet-voiced [6] clouds
That come wind-wafted from Himālaya's height.'

Here the first six lines are an avowed quotation from, and amplification of *Tiruvaḷḷuvar's* fine couplet :[7]

Who every good have killed, may ruin flee;
Who benefit has slain, shall ne'er 'scape free.[8]

This king, who (we may infer) possessed considerable ability, was both brave and generous; but somewhat headstrong. Hence a great deal of good advice is, in a very tactful way, offered to him by the minstrels; and he seems to have been all the better for it. The following lines are worth noting. They are by the same sweet singer.

Good Counsel for the young King.
The Tamiḻ Lands.

[35.]

The pleasant Tamiḻ lands possess
For boundary the ocean wide.
The heaven, where tempests loud sway not,
Upon their brow rests as a crown.
Fertile the soil they till, and wide.

Three kings with mighty hosts this land
Divide; but of the three, whose drums
Sound for the battle's angry strife,
Thou art the chief, O mighty one!

---

[5] The idea that any deeds, good or bad, once done, have thenceforth a real existence, and are among the abiding, active, ever operative energies of the universe, is of primary importance. (See my *Nāl.* pp. 66-69; and *Kuṟaḷ*, Ch. XXXVIII.)

[6] The voice of the rain-cloud is peculiarly the sweet promise of plenty to lands depending solely on the monsoon.

[7] Book I., 'on Virtue,' Ch. XI. 110.

[8] This establishes the priority of the K. to the P. N. N.—Comp. also Nāladiyār, 111 (and note there), 344, 356, 357 (and esp. lex. to Nāl. under root *kol*).

Though the resplendent sun in diverse quarters rise;
And though the silvery planet to the south decline;
Thy land shall flourish, where through channels deep,
Kāveri flows with bright refreshing stream,
Along whose banks the sweet cane's white flowers wave
Like pennon'd spears uprising from the plain.

Let me speak out to this rich country's king!
Be easy of access at fitting time, as though
The lord of justice sat to hear, and right decree.
Such kings have rain on their dominions at their will!
The clouds thick gather round the sun, and rest
In vault of heaven:—So let thy canopy
Of state challenge the sky, and spread around
Not gloom, but peaceful shade! Let all thy victories
Be the toiling ploughman's gain!
Kings get the blame, whether rains fail, or copious flow,
And lack the praise: such is the usage of the world.

If thou hast marked and known this well,
Reject the wily counsels of malicious men.
Lighten the load of those who till the soil.
The dwellers in the land protect. If thou do this
Thy stubborn foes shall lowly bend beneath thy feet.

At one time this king besieged *Karūr*, the C'ēran's capital. The bard of *Ālattūr* ('Fig-tree Town') thus intercedes for the sorely straitened people.

Tactful Intercession for Weak Adversaries.

[36.]

Whether thou wilt destroy or wilt release,
'Tis thine to ponder which befits thy name!—
The axe, bright-edged, long-handled, sharp by file
Of smith black-handed, smites the fragrant boughs
Of guardian trees in every park around;
They crashing fall and scatter the white sands
Of *Ān-porunthamˈs* river cool, where sport
The damsels with their golden bracelets gay;

Thro' town, and all the guarded hall are echoes heard,
And yet their king in pleasure slumbers on!
With bow-armed host, thy war-drum sounding loud,
'Twill shame thee to have fought such feeble foes!

The intercession was unsuccessful; the fair city fell.

The following is by *Nappaçalaiyār of Mārokkam,** seven of whose are songs in this anthology. His grief for its destruction is evident.

Karūr.

[37.]

Thou scion of the C'oḷa Lord who saved
The dove from woe,—Chief of the wrathful hosts,
Armed with the gleaming darts that ruin work,
As when a fiery dragon, angry, fierce,—
Bearing five heads, with gleaming poisonous tooth,
Has enter'd cavern vast mountain, where
The golden creepers twine; fire from the sky
That writhes forth issues, and hot thunderbolt;—
Thou saw'st the lordly city old, whose king
Was circled round by girded elephants.
There in dark deep moat the alligators congregate.
In the wide waters of the guarded lake
Are crocodiles that fierce in fight
Dart forth to catch the shadows cast
By gleam of watchman's torch at midnight hour
Its walls like burnish'd copper shone.
This seemed not fair to thee: Thou didst destroy,
For thou in wasting war art mighty, glorious king!

Here is a bit of adroit but somewhat gross flattery by *Mūlam Kiḻār of Āvūr*:—

The C'ōḷa-land preferred to Swarga.

[38.]

O mighty king, lord of the wide array
Whose wavy banners multiform,

---

* A small district near the ancient Koṛkai.

By youthful hill-like elephants borne on,
Seem as the very heaven they swept!
Fire devastates the place on which thou frown'st!
Where thy favouring glance alights gold gleams!
Wer't thou to wish for moon-beams from the sun,
Or sunny radiance from the pallid moon,
Power hast thou to perform thy will!
Wherefore, since we were born and brought up, 'neath thy shade,
What must the goal of our fond aspirations be?
Thus, even in the regions of thy foes,
Do suppliants think upon thy land,—
Since it is thine,—and say,
They who dwell within the blest domains, great Indra's paradise,
In whose soft glades grows golden fruit, their bliss,
Enjoy the fruit of good deeds, and cease from works
Of charity,—*they from their labours rest*;
Nor there are found the rich who give, or poor who ask.
That were no home for us! But all its joys
Are found here *in the C'ōla-land.*[10]

This is a panegyric by *Nappaçalaiyār of Mārōkkam* :—

Vaḷavan's Praise.

[39.]

Descendant of him who to save a dove from grief did'st enter the weighing scale, whose beam was tipped with the carved white tusk of elephant with ponderous foot! Giving in grace was born with thee: and is not thy peculiar praise.

And, when one ponders how thy sires of old destroyed the mighty 'fort suspended in the sky'[11] which foes dreaded to approach, —to slay thy foes is not thy peculiar praise;

---

[10] Vaḷavan is Indra; and his land is Paradise, which, however, it excels; since its king still bestows charitable benefactions.

[11] Muir, IV. p. 223. This attribution to Vaḷavan's ancestor of this feat seems to imply the descent of the king from Mahādeva. This story is different from the Tirupura Samhāra.—J.M.N.]

And since the council of *Uṛaiyūr*, impregnable city of the valiant C'ōḷar, is the abode of Equity ;—Justice is not thy peculiar praise !

O Vaḷavan, swift horseman, whose stout arms are like fortress-bars, whose wreath fills every eye, how then shall I sing thy praises ?

How shall I tell of thy glorious prowess that withered the fadeless Vañji, destroying the C'ēran king with chariot huge of cunning work, who planted his guarded bow-banner on the long gold tipped peaks of Imayam, whose bounds none measure ? [12]

At *Chezarla* in the Karnūl district there is a temple dedicated to *Kapōlēsvaran* (the 'Dove Lord,'—an epithet of Ṣivan). The legend connected with this shrine is briefly as follows :—

"King Sivi, who came from Kashmir, resolved to perform 100 (yāga) sacrifices by which he hoped to gain the realm of Brahmā. The three Ṣivan, Vishṇu and Brahmā, resolved to interrupt the sacrifice and prevent this; and accordingly Vishṇu assumed the form of a dove which Ṣivan as a hunter pursued with his bows and arrows until it took refuge with Sivi, who took it to his bosom, and refused to give it up to the hungry sportsman. At length it was agreed that he should be permitted to ransom the dove by giving an equal weight of his own flesh. The bird was placed in one scale, and Sivi threw portions of his own body into the other; but the disguised gods prevented the scale from turning, till the king, strong in his heroic self-sacrificing love, cut his own body in halves and threw one into the scale. The gods, overcome by this self-devotion, now assumed their proper shapes, and Ṣivan offered the king a new and more beautiful body, and to make him an emperor. He declined all earthly gifts, asking only the bliss of Kailāsa for himself and his

---

[12] This refers to the legend of King Sivi. See a paper in *Madras Government Records (Archæology)*, dated April 30th, 1899, by A. Rea. Esq.

people." Such was the ancestor assigned by the poet to his patron (39, 43, 46)! [13]

The next by *Mūlam Kiḻār of Āvūr* refers to *the destruction of Karūr*, and is a delicate lyric warning the youthful conqueror against arrogance.

[40.]

Thou art the mighty one, who sparing not the guarded fort broke thro' and slew its king and made the yellow gold erewhile his crown anklets to grace, hero! thy conquering foot.

Thy land maintains seven lordly elephants in tiny spot where a little one might lie! [14]

That we may ever see, as now, the necks of thy despisers bend, and those who laud thee raise their heads, be thou, great king! pleasant of speech, and easy of access." [15]

This is by *Kōvūr Kiḻār*, a sweet singer and friend of many kings. No less than 15 of his compositions are in this collection. Of these, No. 47, '*The Intercession*,' addressed to another chief, is most noteworthy.

'*The Terrors of Invasion*

[41.]

E'en death must bide his time. You choose your own,
O king, and slay whene'er and wheresoe'er
It pleases you: so fall the mighty lords of spearman-hosts!
At all eight points the fiery meteors fall away;
From lofty trees the leafless branches droop;
On every side fierce meteor-ṣuns blaze forth;
Voices of evil-omened birds are heard;

---

[13] The outlines of this story are found in a Buddhist *Jātaka*. See Fausboll, Vol. III. pp. 224-227.—It is given in the *Mahābārata, Vana-parvan*, 13275, etc. And here it is mentioned as connected with an ancestor of a C'ōḻa king. To extract history from such sources is impossible. [The C'ōḻa is reputed as the descendant of the solar line. Hence the reference.—J.M.N.]

[14] i.e., is amazingly fertile. [15] See Kuraḷ, 525, 548, 565.

Teeth fall to earth ; oil drips upon men's heads ;
The wild boar rushes forth ; garments fall to earth ;
Bright weapons with their stands are overturn'd ;
Things rarely seen in dreams, never in waking hours,
O valiant warrior, wait upon thy warlike path !
When rumour of thy dreaded coming spreads,
Dwellers in town unguarded, panic struck,
Kiss their children's flowerlike eyes, and haste
To hide their boding sorrows from their wives ;
And all the people frighted flee.
O Vaḷavan, thou hero in the strife,
Thy march is like the fire before the mighty wind !
So fares the land that hath provoked thy wrath.

Nine portents alarm the people whose lands are invaded. These are the evil omens still dreaded in India.

The following is by *Iḍaikāḍanār* (= 'he of the herdsman's forest land ') :—

The Warrior-king.

[42.]

Insatiate giver ! Lord of murderous war !
Thine elephant looms like a lofty hill ;
Thy warring hosts roar like the billowy sea ;
Thy pointed spear gleams like the lightning's sheen ;
Thus art thou cause of trembling to earth's kings.
No blame to thee, 'tis thine ancestral way !
As tiger guards its whelps thou guardest us,
Safe 'neath thy sceptre just, thou Lord of festive land,
Whose homesteads flourish mid the genial soil.
The reapers from the border-sluices draw rare fish ;
The ploughmen turtles in the furrows find ;
The cutters of the cane rich honey bring ;
The maidens at the fountains lilies cull ;
To feast their kinsfolk from less favour'd fields.
Like many rivers rushing from the hill
From far converging towards the mighty deep

The tuneful bards all turn their eyes to thee.
Thou smit'st with axe whose blows no healing know,
Thine eyes regard the lands of hostile kings
With wrath, as though death's self were raging there!

A chieftain called *Malayamān* (probably the same that goes by the name of *Kāri*—see 121, etc.) fell under Kiḷḷi-Vaḷavan's displeasure, and in some way the little sons of the vassal fell into his hands. These he ordered to be killed by having their heads crushed by an elephant to whose tread they were to be exposed,—a cruel, but not uncommon, punishment in S. India in those days.[16] The poet *Kōvūr-Kiḻār* saved them by his intercession (46), nor was this his only successful advocacy. (See 45, 47.)

Thou art of the royal line of him who saved the dove from affliction and many others.
These are children of the race that protects the learned from want, who share their food with the hungry, and under whose fostering care men lead happy lives.
See these little innocents, how first they stood fearing the sight of thine elephants; then, forgetting that, were daunted by the aspect of thy hall; and now stand trembling with troubles ever new!
Hear me, and then follow the promptings of thine own desire!

They were released.

I now give a specimen of the class of songs called *Āṟṟu-paḍai*, or introduction of a suppliant to a generous patron. The bard is supposed to meet the mendicant in the vicinity of the palace, and encourages him to press on.

---

[16] The victim was buried in the earth, the head only protruding and an elephant driven over the spot.

Kindly Sympathy.

[69.]

In thine hand is the faultless lute; thy body is hunger's prey, for there were none to aid! Around thy waist thou wrappest a cloth patched and darned, and moist with sweat, thou needy minstrel!

Around the world with thy want-wasted company hast thou been, and now enquirest of me.

Kiḷḷi-Vaḷavan is he whose host slays on the reeking bloody plain where high banners wave, the tusked elephant,—he who is lord of *Uṟanthai*, whose spear is up-lifted mid the warriors, strenuous invader of foeman's land, wearer of hero's wreath, and adorned with fire-flashing gems of various hues and ornaments of ruddy gold! Go to his presence! Thou wilt suffer no waiting before the gate.

And when thou him sees't face to face, who in open day [17] gives chariots to those that ask, still less shalt thou lack the lotus wreath around which no beetles swarm.[18]

The next is of the same character :—

[70.]

Minstrel, with little lute of sweetest strain
Suppliant with words of old wisdom full!
Importunate thou askest me to rest and listen to the pleasant sounds of thy tambourine.[19]
But hear what I shall say!

---

[17] The Com. says the day has 30 *nāḷigai* (Tamiḷ hours of 24 minutes). Of these 10, *i.e.*, from 6 a.m. to 10 a.m., are to be given to duties of domestic life, (See K. Book I.) The next 10, *i.e.*, from 10 a.m. to 2 p.m., are to be devoted to kingly duties; and the last 10, *i.e.* from 2 to 6 p.m., being the heat of the day, would be spent in giving audiences and dispensing gifts.

[18] It is of gold!

[19] 'Which has bright face and is fastened to a rod, as turtle from the tank is strung on iron skewer!'

The modest homes of *Pāṇan*,[30] whose hands are full of gifts, is near the wide city.

There food inexhaustible is found like the waters of the cool tank under January's moon, and the humming bees explore the sweets of the fragrant water-lily.

There he meditates the praise and glory of Kiḷḷi-Vaḷavan, king of the good land that yields, in abundance, rice and sweet water, and that knows the fire that cooks, but not the fire that consumes.

If thither,—together with thy songstress, whose hair diffuses fragrance of the 'trumpet-flower,' the bright-browed, sweetly smiling,—you softly advance, you shall prosper well.

His gifts are not mere chance, like gold found by the woodman in the forest.

Hesitate not.

Long may he flourish!

The Hill-Chieftain, 'Strong-bow.'

One of the seven celebrated generous chieftains of the old Tamiḷ country was *Val-vil-ori, or Āthan-ori ('Strong-bow')*. His title expresses his special characteristic: he was a Nimrod, 'a mighty hunter.' His hill was *Kolli*, on the Malabar coast—a hill from which the C'era (or Malabar) kings take one of their titles. He was also celebrated for his lavish gifts of richly caparisoned elephants. Three songs are inscribed in his praise (152, 153, 204).

This chief is mentioned in the *Pattu-pāṭṭu* as having fought with another of the seven liberal kings, *Kāri* (of whom we shall hear by-and-bye). He is also named in 158, but simply as the 'Lord of the gleaming hill of Kolli.'

His especial bard was *Van-Paraṇar*, whose lyric we translate in a somewhat condensed form. It is doubtless a fair picture of the old Tamiḷ highland chiefs before the Muhammadan invasion.

---

[30] Seems a play on the name Paṇṇan.

The Generous Archer.

[152.]

What artisan thy arrows excellent
Fashioned with many a stroke, O thou, in chase
Victorious ever with thy mighty bow ?
Low lay they mighty elephants, and slay
Tigers with wide cavernous jaws,
And spotted antelopes with branching horns !
Before them falls the woodland boar's huge head,
The guano, neighbour of the lowly ant,
They kill. Yet *Ori* hunts not for mere gain,—
Destroyer mighty though he be ; for he
Reigns the right wealthy *Lord of Kolli's* fruitful hill
Around whose base the mountain streamlets flow,—
Whose mighty breast chaplets of pearl adorn.
O minstrel maid, sing thou a triumph-song !
And ye, bear burthen with your tambourines.
Make ready lute and lyre, tabor and drum,
And every instrument of joyous melody !
Then will we pass from land to land, and say :
'There is no huntsman like to him : in war
No arm so strong as his to guard and rule—
The Lord of Kolli's hill, Ori's proud height ;
The brave one, loved and loving, rich in gifts !'

Another bard, whose epithet was 'Owner of the elephant that chews the sugar-cane,' and who is otherwise unknown, has composed an interesting poem in his praise.

The Sea and the Streamlet.

[204.]

'Tis shame to wealthy churls, 'give ye,' to cry ;
Sorer disgrace when these their gifts deny.
Doubtless, who saith, 'Take this my gift,' does well ;
Who saith, 'I take not,' doth in worth excel.
Who thirst for water will not stoop to drink

Where sparkling wavelets play on ocean's brink,—
Tho' draught be crystal clear. Where cattle pass,
And thronging thick make bank a muddy mass,
And tho' the streamlet trickle scant and slow,—
There's well-trod path to where sweet waters flow!
If thou give not, thy suppliants blame the hour
And inauspicious signs, and fate's dread power;—
They blame not thee, as all forlorn they sigh,
For thou art liberal as th' o'er arching sky!

The lavish generosity of the archer-chief is celebrated in hyberbolical strains in 153, which is a singularly artistic Tamiḻ lyric.

Bewildering Munificence.

[153.]

Daily the chieftain of the cloud-crowned hill[21]
Gives askers elephants caparison'd.
Great *Āthan-ori* height,—his hand, adorned
With radiant gems and gold, grasps the round disc,—
Insatiate lover of the deadly strife.
To see his gifts showered down like kindly rain
My merry company went trooping forth
Garlands and ornaments of silver twine,
With jewel-lotus-flowers, in no cool stream
That grew, and line of elephants they gained.
As they went forth, according music loud
Sounded on every side from instruments
Well-strung: but they—because they hungered not?—
Forbore to dance, and quite forgot their song.[22]

These verses give the merest glimpse of the mighty Tamiḻ archer. For twelve centuries they have existed in South India, have been the source of many legends in other literatures, and are mixed up with traditions of the Pāṇḍiyan

---

[21] Kolli.

[22] Paralysed and struck dumb by his munificence.

kings of Madura, who, being supposed to be incarnations of Śiva, had the bow and arrows as their special attributes. But all that is received and accredited tradition about *Ori* is contained in these three lyrics.

After our poet had been treated discourteously by *Velimān's* successor, who offered him a paltry gift which he rejected with scorn, he made his way to Kumaṇan's court, who on this occasion treated him with the utmost cordiality, and presented him with a lordly elephant. With this he made his way back to the palace erewhile belonging to his faithful patron Velimān, but now tenanted by his churlish successor, and tethered his elephant under the trees close to the fort gate. He then revenged himself upon the younger brother, who had occupied the deceased chieftain's seat, by singing the following song. To realise the situation fully we must remember that the bard was considered sacred, and his words of reproach and threatening would surely have effect; while for the present the song was sure to pass from mouth to mouth, and would render the new ruler an object of contempt to some, and of utter detestation to others.

Reproaches.

[162.]

'Thou'rt no protector of the suppliant poor.
Yet to the suppliant kindly friends are ever found.
See here the state of worthy suppliants!
See here the worth of kindly friends!
Behold I tether 'neath the shadow of thy fort
This elephant, another's gift; and so, farewell,
Thou chieftain of the swiftly running steed!'

This does not seem to be a very clever bit of spite; but the reference to the horse here implies an imputation of cowardice, and the tethering his elephant there was a prophecy that the elephants of hostile kings would soon be found in the same spot.

This ever generous *Kumaṇan* was at one period dispossessed of his kingdom by his younger brother and fled to the desert, where he was in great poverty. To him our bard found his way, and sought a gift from the utterly impoverished king. The generous-hearted prince drew his sword and presented it to the suppliant, saying, 'I've nothing to give thee but my head. Cut it off and bear it away!'

The poet took the sword, and made his way back to the court of the usurping brother, where he sang the following song:—

[165.]

'In this fleeting earth some wish to live by fame's report
and so have striven to make their glory last; and they
who still in utmost poverty retain the will to give
to those that ask, are glorious in their woe
I went to him who all has lost but deathless fame! He said.
'I've lost my lands, to bid thee empty go were greater loss
Here is my sword, Take thou my head.' Thus come I from thy
kinsman's presence glad, bearing his sword, sign of his love.'

It is pleasant to know that the issue of this was that the usurper was touched with compunction for having wronged his noble-hearted brother, and restored him his kingdom.

KĀRI, "THE MOUNTAIN CHIEF."

(*Malaiyamān Tirumuḍi-Kāri.*[33])

The *Puṟa-nanūṟu* abounds in short passages of great beauty, casting vivid light upon many old customs, and giving fitting expression to feelings and sentiments which

---

[33] Malaiyamān ("*the mountaineer*" = Malaiyan) is an epithet of the C'era King. Tiru-muḍi = "sacred crown." His domain seems to have been *Malāḍu*, along the banks of the S. Peṇṇār. [Malayamān is an epithet of Kāri himself and not of C'era. Malāḍu is corruption of Malaināḍu. His capital was modern Tirukoilur in South Arcot District. The Patron of St. Sundara ruled there in the 8th century.—J.M.N.]

are common to all the world. Many of these are by Kabilar, the famous poet, of whom a separate notice is given, and who especially sung the praises of the hill chieftains Kāri and Pāri. Kāri was one of the seven minor kings[24] who in latter times were renowned for liberality. It would seem that he was contemporary with Tiru-Vaḷḷuvar. There is some slight discrepancy in the lists, but Malaiyamān, commonly called Kāri (which was really the name of his war-horse), is in every list. Kāri means "blackness," and it seems that the famous charger was called so because of its colour. King Kāri was equally renowned for bravery (having fought as an ally of the Pāṇḍiya, C'oḷa and C'era Kings) and for liberality; but he seems to have been somewhat lavish and indiscriminate in his gifts, as were many of these rude mountain chieftains. Hence Kabilar cautions him :—

[121.]

" Where reigns *one* Lord men's longing eyes are bent
From quarters four they come, on gain intent.
' Tis hard to measure worth ; thy gifts to fling
Abroad with lavish hand is easier thing.
O King munificent ! full well
Thou knowest the very truth I tell.
Cease then to view each suppliant bard
With undistinguishing regard."

In 122, the same poet tells us, that Kāri helped the three great Tamiḻ kings, and that he generously gave the spoils to his own people, so that nothing remained to himself but his queen.

" Thy Queen, pure as the Northern Star,"[25] to matrons shown,
Sweet voiced, is all, great King, thou call'st thine own."

---

[24] கடைஎழுவள்ளல்.

[25] Arunddhati, the chaste wife of Vasishṭha, now a star in Ursa Major, pointed out to brides as an example.

In 123, Kabilar tells us, in a pretty little distich, that he gave chariots as presents, not simply amid the excitement of a feast, but calmly: these gifts were as numerous as the drops of rain that fell on the Mullūr hills. This last reminds us that abundance of rain—the greatest of blessings to Indian cultivators—was ensured by a generosity like his: "It is twice blest, it blesseth him that gives and that receives."

In 124 we hear Kabilar again:—

[124.]

"Suppliant in unauspicious hour,
Mid threatening evil omens' power.
In luckless time they seek his feet!
And though they utter words unmeet,
None empty go away who sing
The praises of the mighty king,
Adown whose mountain[26] steeps the torrent's wrath,
In thunders seeks its long established path."

In 126 another bard called *Nappacalaiyār*, sings the praises of Kāri in much the same strain, but takes care to add that he himself is no rival of Kabilar, "the Brahman of faultless learning," whom he evidently recognises as the court ministrel and Poet Laureate of *Kōvalūr*.[27]

[126.]

"Descendant of the Mighty One
Who tore the gold from off the head
Of foemen's warring elephants,
And made it shining ornament for minstrels' brows!
Who wear'st a glorious wreath of fadeless lotus flowers,
Who knows not flight in war!
To sing thy praise we come, or learned or unlearn'd,—
Lord of the Mount *Mullūr*, upon whose slopes
The forest rest, dark as though night
Gathering her shades around her slumbered there.

---

[26] This was called *Mullūr-Malai*.

[27] Or Kōval. This was Kāri's capital, now Covelong (?) 20 miles S. of Madras. [No. It is the Modern Tirukoilur.—J.M.N.]

May'st thou flourish with thine undecaying race!
The learned Brahman bard, whose praise
Is known to all the sons of men on earth,
The bard with faultless learning graced, hath sung Thy fame,
So that no room remains for any of the suppliant train.
No rival bard, I sing! We're little barks
That sail not on the Western main,
Where C'eran's warlike fleets are seen.
Our poverty compels we add our mite of praise
To him Lord of the fertile land!
On *Peṇṇai* banks where thy war-drums sound out
Like the loud thunder, scaring mountain-snakes.
And where Thou drivest back the tide of foemen's war,
While lordly elephants and kings bestrew the field."

This ends the praise of the 'Highland chief':—

Malayan the victor, who on Kāri rode,
stalwart in war, whose gifts were as the drops of rain!" (158)

Although Perum C'ittiranār was a great favourite with various kings, he seems to have had difficulty at times in eking out a scanty subsistence for himself and family, and the most telling lyrics exhibiting the pains and privations of poverty that we have ever met with, are in this collection under his name. The following may serve as a specimen:—

[159.]

'When will my life expend itself? The years
unceasingly flow on!—Thus she complains,
groping her feeble way with staff in hand.
Her cheeks are thin, wrinkled like skeins of thread.
She in the courtyard sleeps. Thus is it with my mother old![88]
My tenderly beloved wife is wan and worn.
Her starving infants cling around her empty breasts and wail.
Our food is bitter herbs. We heard thy praise,—
our hearts leaped up, were glad as thirsty soil when clouds
big with the rain o'ershadow them; and so we came
singing thy praise,—I and my kin with wasted forms.

---

[88] Nāladiyār 14, 17.

Yet though I were to gain a mighty elephant
with shining tusks, I take not gift thrown me in scorn.
Shouldst thou with pleasure give a courteous boon,
though small as *Kundri*[89] berry, grateful I receive.
O Kumaṇan, whose spear is keen. This is the boon that, praising
thee, I wait.

In some of the famine camps this picture has been a myriad times beheld, and it vividly brings back scenes with which the writer was but too familiar in days by-gone.

The following song of Perum C'ittiranār, who had obtained a handsome gift from Kumaṇan, shows him in an amiable light. It is addressed by the bard to his wife :—

Let all share!

[163.]

All those who loved thee,—all whom thou dost love,—
Thy kindred all, with seemly virtues crowned,
All who in times gone by, thy wants relieved,—
Call them together now; bid all the world!
Nor counsel nor direction ask of me!
Thus will we live, ponder no more,
give thou to all, my housewife dear!
The lord of Muthiran's fruitful hill,
Kumaṇan, Lord of the mighty spear
hath given this wealth, which ALL SHALL SHARE!

The great friend of this ancient king was Paṇṇan (alluded to in Songs 70 and 388 also) who is known only as a petty chieftain of *C'iṟu-Kudi* (Little-town). In regard to such friendships the reader may compare Pope's *Nālaḍiyār*, p. 135. In honour of this friend the king himself composed the following curious little song :—

Paṇṇan's Abode.

[173.]

May *Paṇṇan* happy live as long as I enjoy this life.
See here, ye bards, this suppliant hither makes his way

---

[89] Kuṟaḷ, 965.

By poverty compelled he listens for the sound of food dispensed.
Like to the birds that congregate upon the fruitful tree
In fertile soil, the suppliants come, in ranks,
Crowding like tiny ants that, when they know
The rainy season nigh, bear off their eggs
To some dry, favoured mound.—Although they see
The tribes with all their little ones advance
In thronging multitudes, again and yet again they seek
The dwelling of the man who heals the sore disease of penury.
'Ah tell us is it near or far,' they cry!

Here *King Vaḷavaṉ* is surrounded by singers themselves, suppliants in his court. To them he speaks of the generosity of his friend Paṇṇan, and blesses him. Then he points to an ideal picture of what may constantly be seen on the road to Paṇṇan's home, where, when the drum proclaims the feast to which all are welcome, crowds gather like the birds on every fruitful tree, while on the slope of the hill below his palace suppliants ask of those whom they meet returning satisfied and happy, in continuous train like the ants,—'tell us how far it is to the dwelling of the generous chieftain for whose aid we seek: the healer of hunger's sore disease.' This illustrates, as do very many other songs in this anthology, the state of things in those days in the petty kingdoms of the South. Organised bands of mendicants,—some of them poets, reciting their elaborate compositions,—often most ingenious, and sometimes quite beautiful, but full of fulsome and far-fetched adulation,—some of them musicians with all kinds of quaint instruments,—with bands of female singers and dancers, were perpetually making their way to and fro from one little mountain fortress to another, where their advent formed one of the few distractions of life for the chieftain, alternating with his hunting expeditions and war-like raids.

The Minor Bards, Perum-Talai-C'āttanār and Perum C'ittiranār.

These wandering minstrels, though quite willing to praise their patrons in the most lavish way, were exceedingly sensitive, and no doubt ofttimes severely tried. The petty hill chieftains and their retainers were not always models of courtesy and refinement, and occasionally kept their suppliants waiting long in suspense, even when they eventually sent them forth laden with rich presents. Sometimes the present was sent, but no personal interview accorded to the slighted poet, who considered himself more than the equal of any mountain chieftain. The warders at the gates of the palaces often refused admission, or allowed it only on the promise of a substantial share of the present obtained. Thus the way of these wanderers was sometimes rough, and in their poems they were not slow in giving very decided expression to their feelings.[30]

---

[30] Those that are acquainted with Mr. Lowell's exquisite poem of Sir Launfal will be surprised at the resemblance it bears in parts to various Tamil lyrics.

This poem turns on the idea that the value of the gift depends upon the disposition of the giver. Sir Launfal tossed a piece of gold in scorn to the leper as his alms.

" The leper raised not the gold from the dust:
' Better to me the poor man's crust,
Better the blessing of the poor,
Though I turn me empty from his door;
That is no true alms which the hand can hold;
He gives nothing but worthless gold
Who gives from a sense of duty;
But he who gives a slender mite,
And gives to that which is out of sight,
That thread of the all-sustaining Beauty
Which runs through all and doth all unite,—
The hand cannot clasp the whole of his alms,
The hand outstretches its eager palms,

There were two minor poets of somewhat similar characters and fortunes in whose verses there is naturally considerable resemblance, both of whom were exceedingly sensitive, and expressed their disgust at the unfeeling and uncourteous way in which they were treated.

It may be said, by the way, that, on the other hand these ancient chieftains must very often have been sorely tried by their numerous, arrogant and very pertinacious suitors.

The following is by the first of these bards, *Perum-Talai-C'ăttanăr*. He is addressing a chieftain, a wild huntsman of whom nothing more is known, who delayed his gift, and was utterly wanting in cordiality:—

A somewhat defiant Plea for kindly Charity.

[205.]

'Though the three monarchs rich in amplest wealth,
gave loveless gifts, we'd scorn the pelf!
O Lord of Kovai, round whose heights,
the jasmine twines its wreaths all glittering white,
whose sword victorious quenches ardour of thy foes,
whilst thou to needy suppliants that flee
to thee from face of conquering foes, art refuge sure!
O huntsman searching out from rocky cave,

For a god goes with it and makes it store
To the soul that was starving in darkness before.'

Afterwards, Sir Launfal, having learnt the lesson, shared his crust with the same leper, and gave him water in his own cup from the stream. And the moral is.—

'*Not what we give, but what we share,—*
For the gift without the giver is bare.'

We venture to suggest to the educated youth of South India this poem of Sir Launfal as an exceedingly fitting one for translation, or transfusion, into Tamil. [I took up the suggestion of Dr. Pope and I got Mr. T. Veerabadra Mudaliar, B.A., B.L., to translate this poem into Tamil and it was published in Siddhānta Dipikā, Vol. IV. p. 62 et seq.]

and den all creatures great and small, with hounds
swift-footed, bearing still thy mighty bow!
May thy blest days in joyous comfort pass!
The clouds that go to graze on Ocean's plain
drink from its plenteous store, nor ever back
come they without the gift they seek ;—
so suppliants, from thee, or from some other, gain
Due gift of car and tusked elephants.!

[*I. e., 'Farewell, if you give not, some other will be more kind.*]

In several other pieces much the same topics are brought forward ; but his death is the theme of those that follow. This took place at *Kuḷamuṟṟam*. Tamiḷ kings are distinguished in legend sometimes by some victory gained, but oftener by the place of their death, or slumber, as it is called (*tuñju*='fall asleep').

How Death secured his Victim.

[226.]

If in his mind against thee he were wrath,
Or if in outward act he showed his rage,
Or if he touched thee with afflictive hand,
Thou couldst not have escaped, O death!
Thou took'st great *Vaḷavan*, entreating him,
Like minstrels, bowing low, with suppliant hand,
Praising, thou didst bear off his life,
Leader of hosts that crowd the glorious field,
Crowned with gold wreath, Lord of the mighty car!

Death would have been unequal to the contest with the valiant king, and only managed to take his life by appealing to his generosity.

Another song by *Māçattanār of Āḍu-tuṛai* commemorates his death, using a quaint old commonplace of Tamil verse. (Comp. 230).

Death's Want of Foresight.

[227.]

Death! Right silly art thou, ruthless one;
Through lack of sense thou eat'st thine own seed-corn!
Thou yet shalt see the truth of what I say.
Warriors with gleaming swords, and elephant and horse
Fell on the battle-plain that flowed with blood;
Daily he was insatiate, slew his foes,
And fed thine hunger! Like thyself a strength
He had that knew no ruth nor vengeance feared
This *Vaḷavan* who wore the mighty golden ornaments,
Whose flowery garland swarmed with humming bees,
Since thou hast borne away,—who shall appease thine hunger now?

These verses refer to *Vaḷavan's funeral*, and is attributed to *Muḍanār* (=the lame bard) *of Aiyūr*:

The Burial-urn.

[228.]

'O potter-chief![31] maker of vessels!
Thou whose furnace sends up thick clouds
Of smoke veiling the outspread heavens,
Who makest vessels for the wide extended ancient town!
Thou art to be pitied! What toil hath befallen thee!
The descendant of C'ōla kings,
Whose armies spread themselves to earth's utmost verge,—
Whom minstrels praise,—the truly glorious one,—
Whose glory shines afar,
As in the heavens the sun with resplendent ray,—
Vaḷavan, the great, on the brows
Of whose warrior-elephants bright banners wave,—

---

[31] The common words Kuya-van (Kuça-van) for 'potter' are all connected with S. *ku, kô gô*. See *Maṇi-mê*, 28, 34.

Hath gained the world of gods. And so
'Tis thine to shape an urn, so huge
That it shall cover the remains of such an one.
But if thou'st mould the needful urn, thy wheel,
The vast earth must be, and Mêru's mass
Sufficeth not for earth to mould its form!'

Bishop Caldwell says that at the time when these urns were used cremation must have been unknown, and burial the universal practice; but, in fact, the two customs have ever existed side by side. The ancient inhabitants of the South generally buried their dead, as will be seen by a careful study of Puṟa-Poruḷ-Veṇbā; but Brāhmanical and Śaivite usages were found side by side, from very early times. In fact, the oldest funeral hymn, *Rigveda*, X. 18, might well seem to be one of these lyrics. It will be seen also by a reference to the two works already named (which are a perfect mine of information regarding the ancient manners and customs of the southern lands), and from passages scattered through the other Tamiḻ classics, that when heroes fell in battle they were often buried on the spot and their effigies in stone placed over the grave. The same was done when kings and other great men retired into some lonely region (generally specified as the 'North'), and died there. This is exemplified, as we have seen,[32] in the very touching histories of the king *Kō-perum-çōḻan* and his devoted friends *Pottiyār* and *Piçirōn*. This illustrates *Kuṟaḷ* ch. lxxviii. 1.

'Ye foes! stand not before my lord! for many a one
Who did my lord withstand now stands in stone!'

Here the learned commentator, *Parimêlaḻagar* remarks that when heroes died on the field of battle, it was the custom to place their effigies on the spot where they fell. These heroes often became tutelary divinities, or demons, and were worshipped with offerings of food and flowers.

---

[32] *Ind. Ant.* Feb. 1899.

In the *Records* of the Madras Government (Archæological Department) under date 12th May, 1887, an account is given of *vessels discovered at Pallāvaram*, which evidently had been used for burial. These are precisely what this lyric speaks of.[38] Many of the articles of pottery found in connection with these kists may be accounted for by the well-known customs referred to in P.N.N. 234, 249.

Another mountain chief of the same period, if indeed we can form any opinion about the where and when of many of these personages, was *Velimān*, who was very liberal, and who had at least one faithful friend, the poet Perum-C'ittiranār.

Of Velimān himself nothing is known. The minstrel came to his court to find his patron dead, and the successor seems to have treated him with contempt; probably as the heir he had felt grieved at the manifold largesses of the chief which had diminished his inheritance. The poet's dirge is a song of despair.

He has gone to wilderness where ruddy urns
are filled with bodies of the dead,—to wilds
where red-eared vultures, owls and fearsome ravens,
birds obscene of every name, and goblins dwell
and wander as they list. He loved the palm-wine jar!
The beauty of the fair whose arms bright jewels lack has faded;
the minstrel band in tarnished glory past away;
the drums that erst spake out are rent;
the hill-like elephants, tusks lost, their riders lack!
Cruel strong death hath thee destroyed,
my father, what shall happen next I know not, I—
object of pity am I come. What will befall my kin?
In darksome night tempestuous sinks my bark
amid the waves; and like our blind and dumb,
with mind o'erwhelmed in sore distress I see the billows

---

[38] See my article in J. R. A. S., April, 1899.

none may mete or count. In deep of dark despair I sink
by whirling eddies drawn below. Death is the boon I crave!

(Comp. Nālaḍiyār 12.)

The following (208) is by Perum-C'ittiranār, to whom a gift had been offered by Avvai's friend and patron, Athiyamān Neḍumān Añji, but an interview with the king was not allowed, and in fact no civility was shown the perhaps over-sensitive poet:—

'O'er many a mountain, many a hill I have come
thinking to get my gift and go. I deemed
that he with gracious speech would come?
confer his gift, and bid me go in peace.
But he, resistless in the fight, my worth
how did he estimate? I am no mercenary mendicant
that he should give me gifts, yet never see my face!
He should have cherished me, and though his gifts
were small as millet seed, if given with pleasant glance
and words of kindly courtesy, the gift were sweet.'

[386.]

In the following verses, *Kôvūr-kiḻār* seems to stimulate rather than restrain the young chieftain in his gay and thoughtless time:—

'Glory be thine, O giver, whose brow knows no sweat
From labour done, but only that from eager feasting!—Like drops of rain
That fall in the full lake, drips down the fat
From the meats they serve up; roasted flesh is
Carved and eaten; from their emptied porringers they
Quaff large draughts of milk!—
Thy fields of rice,—wide are their borders, where
The sweet cane flowers! Thy pasture lands,—with stalls
For herds,—there cattle graze!
Archers with fortified camps guard the flocks, and from the
Tree-tops on the wooded shore count the ships that cover thy sea!—

In the bay, they load the abounding salt with which thy craggy mountains teem!
To thee, warrior chief, we come,—no warriors we!
Whether from East to West, or from West to East, or
From North to South, or from South to North, thou win
Thy everwidening way;—may his glory shine,
Who knows well to extend his conquests in every land!'

The following ode to the same hero is by an unknown bard called *Nalliṟaiyanār*. It is very imperfect in the original, and is here considerably abridged. To the student of Tamiḻ it is of considerable interest.

[393.]

'O king, I come from far,
With soul that thinks of thee,
And says, "What kindly ones in other lands
Are there to fill the empty dish
Borne by my spouse in sorrow, while with me
She sings, and begs from door to door,
In poverty unknown before.
With thee shall we obtain new garments for the old
Bright as expanding leaves of the *paganrai*,[**] flower;
And feast, departing rich in gifts.
Lord of the beauteous land *Kāveri* guards!
So shall we praise in varied song thy might
Renowned, and say, may *Vaḷavan* whose sword is sharp,
Flourish for aye!"'

A very remarkable lyric addressed to him, presumably at this period of his greatest glory, is by *Tāyam Kaṇṇanār*, of Erukaṭṭur, a poet otherwise unknown. It forcibly recalls *Māṇikka Vāçagar's* fine 'Morning Hymn in the Temple.' [*Tiruvāçagam*, XX.]

[**] The same as the *çinthil*: *Menispermum cordifolium*.

The King's Reveil.

[397.]

The morning-star with silver radiance bright
Now fills the ample sky, and waking birds
From out their nests on lofty boughs send forth
Sweet sounds. On the lake's surface lotus-flowers
Have open'd wide their eyes ; and one by one
The stars now slowly quench their golden fires.
And while the morning drum is sounding loud,
And shrill-ton'd winding shell its summons gives,
Swift on the yielding steps of fleeing night
The eager day triumphant presses on !
Come forth, O king, to view thy mustering hosts !
List to the morning uprise in the guardian camp,
Where sheen of spears dispels the hovering shades.
King, on whose breast hang wreaths of clustering flowers !
And hear the drummer at the outer gate !
He bids thee from thy slumber wake. I come
A suppliant, who loves to see thy state,—
Thou who dost give rich food with spices blent,
And palm-wine fragrant cool, in jewell'd flask,
With garments bright as when a snake its skin renews :—
Thus, showering blessings in thy bounty, like the rain
Thou dost with costly gifts relieve my pain,
That burnt like glow of scorching summer-sun.
Lord of the land where ever shine the fires
Lit by the sages, who six works perform,—
Around their brows the ruddy lotus wreathed,—
And virtue's work maintain ; great *Valavan*,
Whose strong right arm with golden circlets bound
Wields the sharp sword ! Tho' we to farthest bound
Of the vast billowy sea should go ; or tho'
The orb whose rays destroy should southward stray,
We nothing dread ! beneath the mighty foot,—
That wears the hero's glorious jewelled band,—
Of him, whose conquering spear in arduous fight
Prevails, we rest secure.